CALIBAMA COOKING

Chef Lorious

CALIBAMA COOKING

CLASSIC & CONTEMPORARY COMFORT FOOD

Chef Lorious

CHEF LORIOUS
MEDIA, LLC

Published by Chef Lorious Media, LLC

Copyright © 2020 Lori Rogers

All rights reserved. No part of this book may
be reproduced, stored, or transmitted by any
means—whether auditory, graphic, mechanical, or
electronic—without written permission of the publisher,
except in the case of brief excerpts used in
critical articles and reviews. Unauthorized reproduction
of any part of this work is illegal and is punishable by law.
Send inquires to Info@ChefLorious.com

ISBN: 978-1-7340325-0-5 (Hardback)

Photo credits: Stephanie Ascari, title page, vi, x, 5, 68, 93, 154, 157, 169, 180; Jack Gutirrez, 8–9, 30, 39, 76, 97, 103, 111, 145, 150, 177, 214, 243, 251; Mobile Alabama on USA map Shutterstock © Cenz07 and Sacramento on USA map Shutterstock © Alexander Lukatskiy, xii.

Book Design by DesignForBooks.com

Printed in the U.S.A.

DEDICATION

This book is dedicated to my best friend, my confidante, and my love; the man who always believes in me and always has my back; the man who knew I could do it before I even believed it was possible—to my amazing and incredible husband, Shane. I love you. Thank you for always seeing me and loving me authentically.

To my children, Richard, Madison, and Aiden: thank you for being patient with Mommy and for tasting every dessert I make. It's a tough job, but somebody's gotta do it!

To my mother: thank you for always making sacrifices with my best interest in mind. You've been there from Day 1, and I couldn't accomplish anything without your support.

CONTENTS

Introduction   1

Where the Magic Happens: The Love Lab   5

SMALL PLATES AND STARTERS   7

Buffalo Chicken Taquitos   9

Chipotle Deep-Fried Macaroni-and-Cheese Balls   11

Bacon Guacamole   13

Sweet and Salty Baked Brie   15

Steak-and-Cheese Egg Rolls   17

Super Bowl   19

Sweet and Spicy Asian Wings   23

Smoky Spinach Dip   25

Calibama Corn Fritters   27

Chimichurri Steak Nachos   29

Summer BBQs   31

Tangy Broccoli Salad   35

Shrimp Po'Boy Dip   37

SOUPS, CHOWDERS, AND STEWS   39

Baked Potato and Bacon Soup   41

Corn, Bacon, and Potato Chowder   43

Sausage Tortellini Soup with Spinach   45

Spicy Seafood, Chicken, and Sausage Stew   49

Beef Stew   53

Calibama Chili   55

Chicken Pot Pie   59

Guinness Shepherd's Stew   61

Turkey Tortilla Soup   63

MAIN COURSES   65

Rosemary Seared Chicken Thighs   67

Lorious Chicken and Waffles   69

Dip Dinners   71

Garlic Cream Chicken   75

Garlic and Brown Sugar Pork Tenderloin   77

Hearty Chicken Piccata   79

Beef and Sausage Meatloaf   81

Lori's Meaty Marinara Sauce   85

Beef Stroganoff   87

Crab-Topped Filet Mignon   89

The Love of My Life   91

Easy Everyday Beef Wellington   95

Herb-Crusted Prime Rib   99

Country Fried Steak and Gravy   101

Mother's Day   105

Lamb Chops in Madeira Wine Sauce   107

Sausage-Stuffed Portobello Mushroom Caps   109

Pork Enchiladas Verde   113

Smothered Pork Chops   117

Extra Meaty Hearty Lasagna   121

Lemon Basil Chicken   123

Cajun Chicken Pasta   125

SEAFOOD   127

Fish Fries   129

Pan-Seared Swordfish with Greek Sauce   131

Creamy Cajun Lobster and Shrimp Fettuccine   133

Blackened Salmon with Lemon Herb Butter   137

I Love Me Some Grits   139

Spicy Shrimp and Grits   141

Crab-Stuffed Flounder   143

Lobster and Shrimp Rolls   147

Cilantro Lime Shrimp Tacos   149

SIDES AND VEGGIES   151

Lorious Macaroni and Cheese   153

Refined Little Palates   155

Sautéed Cabbage with Bacon and Garlic   159

Lucky Black-Eyed Peas   161

Grandma's Collard Greens   163

Crispy Glazed Brussels Sprouts   165

Thanksgiving   167

Sausage and Mushroom Dressing   171

Garlic and Herb Potato Stacks   173

Mama's Potato Salad   175

Mama's Potato Salad   179

SWEET STUFF   181

Classic 7UP Cake   183

Sweet Potato Pie   185

Bourbon Peach Cobbler   187

Chocolate Lava Cake   189

Maddie's Apple Caramel Cobbler   191

Nana Jo's Old-Fashioned Lemon Pie   195

Pumpkin Brown-Sugar Pound Cake   199

Old-Fashioned Rice Pudding   203

Banana Pudding   205

White Chocolate Crème Brûlée   207

Bake-Sale Pies   211

Coconut Cream Pie   213

Lemon Meringue Pie   215

Chocolate Bread Pudding with Irish Whiskey Caramel Cream Sauce   217

Chocolate Waffles   221

Chocolate Chip Skillet Cookie   223

Ooey-Gooey Cast-Iron Chocolate Caramel Brownie   225

Lori's No-Mess Perfect Piecrust   229

Meringue   231

BREADS   233

Garlic Herb Cheese Bread   235

Zesty Lemon Blueberry Scones   237

I Need Some Strength   241

Sweet Buttermilk Corn Bread   245

Buttermilk Biscuits   247

Pancakes   249

Buttermilk Pancakes   253

Lemon Stuffed French Toast   255

Red Velvet Waffles   257

Spicy Sausage Gravy and Biscuits   259

About the Author   261

Index   263

My parents (circa 1969)

INTRODUCTION

This cookbook is the intersection of Sacramento, California, and Mobile, Alabama, as recounted in Fairfax, Virginia (where I currently reside).

I was born and raised in Sacramento. My parents are both from Mobile (well, technically, they're from Prichard, but don't worry about that little detail). They grew up probably no more than ten miles apart, but they met and married in California. Their individual journeys to the West Coast were different, but nonetheless, their paths intersected, they married, and they had one child together: me!

My father had a sister whose military husband had landed them in Sacramento. So when my father got out of the navy and was settling down, he headed west too. There weren't many opportunities in the sixties for Blacks in the Deep South, so California seemed like a pretty good option.

My mother and me
(circa 1977)

My maternal grandfather worked for a civilian military base in Mobile that closed in the midsixties. Several of the men in my mother's community worked for the same base. When the base closed, a large group of them opted to relocate to a base in Sacramento. And off they went!

Originally, when my grandparents moved with my mom's younger siblings, she was away at college. As soon as she finished, she joined them in California. Like I said, there weren't a lot of options for Blacks in the Deep South.

Because a large group of Blacks from the same community all came to California in the same period, my mother knew a lot of the folks who she grew up with, and they were a part of my everyday life. My grandfather started a church in Sacramento and a lot of the folks who had migrated from Mobile went to that church, so there was a little Alabama sitting in the middle of Sacramento.

My Grandmother and me (circa 1983)

My life was shaped by that community. I basically had three moms: my mom, my grandma, and my godmother. And there were countless other church ladies around, along with my aunts and uncles. All of these Alabama natives played a key role in my life, and they shaped me into the wife, mother, friend, and woman I have become. Most importantly for today's conversation was their impact on my culinary views. I watched those church ladies cook everything—and I mean everything!

When you're a California native with Alabama influences, you love things like grits and collard greens, and you learn how to make an amazing sweet potato pie. Calibama is the intersection of where I grew up and where I'm really from.

Everybody has a story. Everybody is from somewhere. Our lives represent where we are from, where we are, and where we are going. Every moment in our lives is an expression of the intersection of these points.

There's a delicate balance between reflection and regret. Reflecting on things in our past can make us more grateful for our current situation. It can also bring back painful memories that we'd rather forget. That is the regret portion! But even in the sad memories, there's something to learn, something to hold on to.

Every decision in my life and yours comes from taking the information we have available at the time and making the best decision possible with the current intel. Each experience grows our intel base. While this is quite an undertaking, my story can be told in food . . . well, this part of my story can be told in food.

Some of the recipes are just like what I saw my grandma and the church mothers cooking. Some of them are my interpretation of what happens when a California girl learns to cook from her Alabama family and community.

My story is one of a little girl born into a family full of Southern love and hospitality—a community of people who viewed me as the baby and gave me all of the nurture and consideration that comes with that title. My story continues on to include heartbreak, motherhood, and womanhood. What I've learned is that every experience has made me the woman I am. Every hurt has made me stronger. Every hug has made me love deeper. Every disappointment has made me a little wiser. Every successful collaboration has increased my faith in humanity. Every independent failure has drawn me back to my faith in God. Every win has reminded me just how much He loves me.

My Godmother and me (circa 1973)

All of that is who I am. My food represents those hurts, hugs, disappointments, successful collaborations, and independent failures. At the end of the day, knowing who I am and where I've come from is the foundation for my classic cooking style. Accepting where I am and embracing my future is the stepping-stone for my contemporary interpretation of what true comfort food is: food that makes you comfortable, brings a smile to your face, and reminds you of all the good in the world around you.

My husband actually coined the word *Calibama* when we were dating. I made him dinner one Sunday afternoon: BBQ baked pork chops and collard greens. As he watched me clean and cut up the greens, he asked me very calmly, "Where are you from again?"

I casually answered, "California."

He responded, "No, no, no, where are your people from?"

I answered, "Oh. Alabama."

He said "That's it! You're from Calibama. 'Cause nobody from California rolls greens like that!"

I hope you enjoy my story, and I hope you see and taste some of your story as well. Your story may not be one of Southern comfort food, but whatever is the authentic representation of you is your story. Here's mine.

WHERE THE MAGIC HAPPENS:
THE LOVE LAB

Some of the best things in life happen by accident. By definition, a laboratory is a place where you experiment and try different things. I enjoy trying things in my kitchen. Sometimes stuff just doesn't work out, but most of the time it does. It is truly no exaggeration for me to say that everything I cook, I cook with love. Even when I'm messing around trying new stuff, it's coming from a place of love.

Now that I think about it, even if something doesn't come out just right, you can still taste my heart in every bite. For all these reasons, I named my kitchen the Love Lab. It's where I create new things and perfect existing recipes. It's where I experiment and discover my family's new favorite meals. It's where I recreate our favorite meals from childhood. It's the nucleus of my home. It's the greatest expression of my heartbeat and individuality. It is, indeed, a Love Lab.

SMALL PLATES AND STARTERS

Every meal ain't a big meal! Sometimes you just want a snack, and sometimes you just want a li'l taste. My littlest baby, Aiden, is a grazer, so in my opinion there are never enough small-plate recipes. Other times, it's nice to have a fancy-dancy appetizer with your meal. Whether you're grazing, looking for party food, or just wanting something to start your meal off right, there are plenty of options for you right here.

BUFFALO CHICKEN TAQUITOS

Makes 15–20 taquitos.

Weekends are made for fun foods, like these crispy and delicious taquitos. These are perfect for game night and movie night. Be sure to make a lot because everyone will be reaching for more!

Directions

1. In a large skillet, heat ½ inch oil over medium-high heat until hot enough to sizzle when you add the rolled taquitos, 5–7 minutes. Test the oil by dropping a small drop of water into the pan. If the water sizzles, the oil is ready.
2. Combine shredded chicken, cream cheese, sour cream, chili powder, and cayenne in a stand mixer. Stir in shredded cheese and cilantro. Add buffalo wing sauce and combine all in mixer. Add salt to taste.
3. Fill each corn tortilla with approximately 1 tablespoon of filling; roll tightly.
4. Place taquitos in frying pan in batches, seam-side down. Fry until golden brown, turning once.
5. Remove taquitos from oil and place on a paper towel to remove excess oil.
6. Serve with additional sour cream.

INGREDIENTS

- neutral oil for frying (such as peanut oil or canola oil)
- 2 cups shredded cooked chicken breast
- 4 ounces cream cheese, softened
- ½ cup sour cream, plus more for serving
- 1 teaspoon chili powder
- 1 teaspoon cayenne pepper (optional)
- 1 cup shredded cheddar jack cheese
- 1 teaspoon cilantro, chopped,
- ¾ cup buffalo wing sauce
- salt to taste
- 20 small corn tortillas

TIPS

★ Corn tortillas give you crispy taquitos. Flour tortillas may be easier to handle because they are more pliable, but they just don't give you that crunch we've all come to expect when eating taquitos.

★ I prefer to fry my taquitos in corn oil instead of peanut oil. Most times, you can't get me to fry with anything but peanut oil, but this is an exception to the rule. I like the flavor the corn oil gives the taquitos. It probably doesn't matter, but for what it's worth, that's my two cents!

★ If you don't have a stand mixer, you can combine the filling ingredients in a bowl, but the stand mixer makes it much easier.

CHIPOTLE DEEP-FRIED MACARONI-AND-CHEESE BALLS

1 can't tell you how many times this appetizer has turned into dinner. I remember one Halloween in particular when this before-trick-or-treating snack turned into much more. I have to be honest: it was way better than ordering pizza!

Directions

1. After preparing macaroni and cheese, add chipotle seasoning and mix well. Allow the mixture to set before proceeding (see tip).

2. Scoop ¼–⅓ cup of set macaroni-and-cheese mixture into your hands. Shape into a ball.

3. Dip ball into egg mixture, then roll in panko mixture. You will need to repeat this process several times for each of the balls. (It's better to have extra panko mixture prepared rather than trying to mix more coating as you go along.)

4. Fill a large stockpot ½ to ⅔ full of oil. Heat the oil over medium-high heat until hot enough to sizzle when you add the balls, 5–7 minutes. Test the oil by dropping a small drop of water into the pan. If the water sizzles, the oil is ready.

5. Place coated balls in hot oil for frying. Fry until golden brown. Be sure to rotate balls in oil to make sure they are golden brown on all sides.

6. Remove balls and place on baking rack, allowing excess oil to drain through to paper towels underneath.

MAKES 15–18 LARGE BALLS

INGREDIENTS

Lorious Macaroni and Cheese

2 tablespoons chipotle seasoning

2 eggs plus 1 tablespoon whole milk, lightly whisked

1–2 cups panko bread crumbs mixed with 1 tablespoon chipotle seasoning

peanut oil for frying

TIPS

★ Allow the mac and cheese to set for a while before shaping into balls. I've tried three different ways to do this: leave the mac-and-cheese mixture on the counter for several hours; place it in the fridge for a couple of hours; or put it in the freezer for 30 minutes to an hour. All three methods work. Which you choose depends on how much time you have.

★ Be sure to season the panko bread crumbs. Don't skip that step; the seasoned coating gets the whole experience off to the right start.

BACON GUACAMOLE

Serves 2–3

*L*et's face it: a party isn't really a party until the guacamole comes out. One of my favorite things about guacamole is that you can make it work for everybody: spicy, mild, or right down the middle.

Directions

1. In a large bowl, mash avocados with a fork.
2. Add shallot, garlic, and cilantro; combine well.
3. Fold in bacon and tomato.
4. Add lime juice, salt, and cayenne. Adjust seasonings to fit your taste. (Just don't eat it all while you're tasting!)
5. Serve with tortilla chips or as an accompaniment to tacos and enchiladas.

INGREDIENTS

2 avocados, peeled, pit removed
2 tablespoons finely chopped shallot or onion
1 tablespoon minced garlic
1 tablespoon chopped cilantro
3 slices bacon, cooked and crumbled
1 medium tomato, diced
juice of half a lime
salt to taste
cayenne pepper to taste

TIP

★ You can use a potato masher to mash the avocados, but fork mashing gives you a more authentic texture in the end (if you're into that sort of thing with avocados).

SWEET AND SALTY BAKED BRIE

Serves 3–4

INGREDIENTS

1 (13-ounce) brie round, halved or quartered

4 tablespoons honey

½ cup pancetta

½ cup pomegranate seeds

1 teaspoon cinnamon

*E*verybody needs an elegant appetizer that says, "I got class!" I think it's impossible to go wrong with brie. It works for dressed-up holiday gatherings and as an opener to a casual cocktail party.

Directions

1. Preheat oven to 350 degrees F.
2. Place brie on a baking sheet lined with aluminum foil, and drizzle generously with honey. (You can use more than my recommended 4 tablespoons if you want it a little sweeter.)
3. Bake for 10–15 minutes, until brie is soft but not oozing out.
4. Meanwhile, in a small skillet, brown the pancetta over medium heat until it is slightly crisp.
5. Remove brie from oven and sprinkle pancetta and pomegranate seeds on top while warm. Sprinkle cinnamon on top and serve with crackers, fresh bread, veggies—whatever you want!

TIPS

★ When baking larger brie rounds, I cover them with foil to ensure the inside gets soft and melts smoothly. You can put your side goodies (pomegranates, nuts, or whatever) directly inside the brie round, or you can add them at the end. Either way, it won't last long!

★ Pancetta is italian bacon. If you can't find it, regular bacon or prosciutto will do.

STEAK-AND-CHEESE EGG ROLLS

Serves 5–6

*E*gg rolls are one of the most versatile foods around. You can pretty much turn anything you like into an egg roll—just stuff, seal, and fry! I love steak and cheese sandwiches, and one day, I figured, why not? The results are priceless.

INGREDIENTS

2 tablespoons olive oil

2 pounds steak, cut into small pieces

3 tablespoons steak seasoning

1 tablespoon garlic powder

salt and pepper to taste

1 large yellow onion, diced

1 cup sliced baby bella mushrooms

2 tablespoons chopped garlic

1 cup shredded cabbage

2 cups shredded provolone cheese

1 pack egg roll wrappers plus 1 small bowl of cold water

neutral oil for frying (such as peanut oil or canola oil)

Directions

1. In a large skillet, heat 2 tablespoons olive oil over medium-high heat.
2. Season steak with steak seasoning, garlic powder, salt, and pepper. Set aside.
3. Add onion, mushrooms, and garlic to the skillet and sauté until they begin to soften. Add extra olive oil if needed to keep the mixture from sticking to the skillet. (Pay attention to the temperature of the oil. Although it was heated over medium-high, you may need to decrease it to medium to be sure you don't burn the onions and garlic.)
4. Add shredded cabbage to the skillet and combine well.
5. Once all veggies have started to soften, add the seasoned steak. Cook all ingredients together until the steak is no longer pink inside. (To test this, remove a small piece of steak and cut it open to see the color inside.)
6. Remove steak mixture from the heat and stir in cheese. The heat from the meat and veggies will melt the cheese.

7. Taste the mixture and adjust seasonings as desired—more garlic powder, salt, pepper, and the like (maybe even a little cayenne!).

8. Place 1–2 tablespoons of filling on each egg roll wrapper. Place filling at an angle.

9. Using your finger, moisten edges of the wrapper with cold water. Fold the egg roll like an envelope. Be sure to connect the seams. The water will make it stick.

10. In another large skillet, heat ½ inch oil over medium-high heat until hot enough to sizzle when you add the egg rolls, 5–7 minutes. Test the oil by dropping a small drop of water into the pan. If the water sizzles, the oil is ready.

11. Reduce heat to medium and add the egg rolls in batches. Fry until golden brown. Start with the seam side down to ensure egg rolls stay sealed.

SUPER BOWL

When my husband and I were dating, we threw a Super Bowl party. It was our first joint-hosted social event, and it was a huge success. We didn't realize how much each of us liked to entertain—how each of us became obsessed with every detail.

That first party had about ten guests—close family and a few friends. Little did we know at the time that we were starting a tradition. Now our Super Bowl party has a life of its own. Dare I say it's one of the most coveted tickets in town? Maybe that's going a little too far! But trust me—you really want to be there if you can.

Here's the key to throwing a good party: think through the whole event and have food for every moment. The Super Bowl is more than just the biggest football game of the year. It's about the game, but it's also about the commercials, the pregame show, the halftime show, the postgame interviews, and of course, the food! You must have plenty of food of all types and varieties.

When a team isn't doing well, fans will need to switch up their plate and try something different. Your job as the host is to ensure that they can fix an entirely new plate with almost none of the same food they had on the first plate. You need celebration food, comfort food, peacemaking food, and some downright decadent options.

Wings tend to be the star of the show. Don't make just one type of chicken wing. What will your friends do when their team misses a field goal? They need a new chicken wing! My rule of thumb is at least three types of wings. (Trust me—there is a method to the madness.)

The Super Bowl is more than just the biggest football game of the year.

There are chili dogs, chili cheese fries, chili cheese nachos, chili burgers . . . the possibilities are endless.

Dips are extremely important too. You need pizza dips, spinach dips, nachos, guacamole . . . you get my point, right? My rule of thumb is five dips. Also, plenty of chips—potato chips, nachos, corn chips, go *all* out! I also like some gourmet dip options, like caramelized onion dip for the white wine guests (you know, the folks who don't like the game, don't watch the game, but come because they know your food is going to be lit). Those folks get tired of chili, meatballs, and pizza.

Speaking of chili, it's multipurpose on Super Bowl Sunday. There are chili dogs, chili cheese fries, chili cheese nachos, chili burgers . . . the possibilities are endless. Be sure you make a big enough pot! This is the event when you pull out your best chili recipe: not the "good" chili but the "OMG this is the best chili I've ever had!" chili. And then there are the all-around appetizers: taquitos, meatballs, chicken tenders, fries, jalapeño poppers, ribs, all the stuff that takes your party to serious legit status.

The point is—don't skimp! Plan your menu, then get on the internet and find five more recipes to add. When it comes to our biggest family events, the Super Bowl and Thanksgiving are at the top of this list.

Whew . . . I'm hungry and tired just thinking about how much I enjoy the Super Bowl!

Actual Super Bowl Party

SMALL PLATES AND STARTERS—**SUPERBOWL**   21

SWEET AND SPICY ASIAN WINGS

*Chicken wings are the quintessential appetizer. I wouldn't be surprised if there was a picture of a wing in the dictionary next to the word *appetizer*!

Directions

1. In a sauté pan over high heat, combine all sauce ingredients. Stir well and bring to a boil.
2. Reduce heat to medium. Let simmer for 20–30 minutes until sauce begins to thicken. Set aside.
3. Preheat oven to 400 degrees F (to bake the wings after frying).
4. In a skillet, heat peanut oil over high heat. Test the oil by dropping a small drop of water into the pan. If the water sizzles, the oil is ready.
5. Place cornstarch in a shallow dish. Season chicken wings with salt and pepper. Add to dish with cornstarch and toss to coat.
6. Add wings to hot peanut oil and fry until golden brown and almost completely done, 5–7 minutes. Remove and toss directly into sauce.
7. When the wings are fully coated in sauce, place on a baking sheet and bake in the oven, uncovered, for 15–20 minutes, until done completely. Test for doneness by sticking a knife or fork into the fattest part of a wing. If the juices run clear, the wing is done.
8. Remove from oven and sprinkle with sesame seeds.

Serves 8–10

INGREDIENTS

For the sauce:

- 3 scallions, chopped
- 1 cup orange juice
- 1 cup pineapple juice
- 1½ cups brown sugar
- ½ cup soy sauce
- ½ cup mirin wine
- 2 tablespoons ginger
- 2 tablespoons minced garlic
- 1 tablespoon red pepper flakes

For the wings:

- peanut oil, for frying
- 1–2 cups cornstarch
- 5 pounds chicken wing drumettes, thoroughly washed and dried
- salt and pepper to taste
- sesame seeds

TIPS

★ You can fry your wings completely and then toss them in your sauce, or fry them until almost done, coat them in sauce, and finish them off in the oven. Either way, they'll be amazing.

★ If you can't find mirin wine, you can substitute a dry white wine mixed with ½ teaspoon sugar for each tablespoon of wine used.

SMOKY SPINACH DIP

This is one of my most requested party appetizers. It's pretty straightforward, but the addition of paprika to the dip as an ingredient, instead of just as a garnish, does amazing things to the flavor. Sometimes subtle is the way to go.

Directions

1. In a medium saucepan over medium heat, melt 5 tablespoons butter. Add garlic and sauté.
2. Add cream cheese and heavy cream and melt in the pan.
3. Stir in Monterey Jack, lemon pepper, lemon juice, and paprika.
4. Rinse the spinach and wring out excess water.
5. In a separate pan over medium heat, melt remaining 2 tablespoons butter. Add spinach and sauté until bright green, about 5 minutes.
6. Stir spinach into cheese mixture; combine well. Add salt and pepper.
7. Serve with french or italian bread wedges, pita chips, or vegetables for dipping.

Serves 6–8

INGREDIENTS

7 tablespoons butter, divided
4 cloves garlic, minced
1 pound cream cheese, softened
1½ cups heavy cream
1½ cups shredded Monterey Jack cheese
1 tablespoon lemon pepper
1 tablespoon lemon juice
1 tablespoon paprika
2½ cups chopped spinach (fresh or frozen and thawed)
salt and pepper to taste

TIPS

★ The dip is ready to eat right out of the saucepan, or you can put it in a baking dish and broil it in the oven for 5–7 minutes. That will allow the top to have a nice light golden color.

★ The paprika gives the dip a smoky flavor, so don't think it's just for aesthetics. It serves a real purpose.

CALIBAMA CORN FRITTERS

Makes 12 fritters

*F*ried corn fritters make a quick small plate that carries quite a punch. Add a dip to balance the heat if you've made them spicy.

Directions

1. In a large skillet (I think cast iron works best), heat ½ inch oil over medium heat.
2. Meanwhile, in a large bowl, combine flour, salt, baking powder, sugar, pepper, and paprika.
3. In a separate bowl, combine milk and egg.
4. Pour egg mixture into flour mixture. Stir to combine. Do not overmix; just get everything incorporated.
5. Add corn and cheese; stir well to combine. Again, do not overmix. Batter should be lumpy.
6. Scoop mixture with a kitchen spoon or small scoop, add to hot oil, and fry fritters in batches for approximately 2–3 minutes on each side until golden brown. (Don't turn the heat up too high, or the fritters will get brown on the outside and still be raw on the inside.)

INGREDIENTS

- neutral oil for frying (vegetable, canola, or peanut)
- 1 cup all-purpose flour
- 1 teaspoon salt
- 1 teaspoon baking powder
- 1 teaspoon sugar
- 1 teaspoon seasoned pepper
- 1 teaspoon paprika
- 1 cup milk
- 1 egg
- 1½ cups corn
- ½ cup grated cheese

TIP

★ You can use either fresh or frozen corn; both work just fine. If using frozen, be sure to fully defrost before frying.

CHIMICHURRI STEAK NACHOS

Serves 6–8

Steak meets chimichurri sauce, goes on a date with nachos, and magic happens. Everything in our house gets amped up by the time I'm done with it, and this is no exception. Dip the nachos in the chimichurri sauce or pour the sauce straight on top—either way, you won't be disappointed.

Directions

1. Marinate the steak in the Brazilian seasonings for at least 30 minutes, or up to 2 hours.
2. Preheat oven to 350 degrees F.
3. Coat the bottom of a skillet (preferably cast iron) with a thin layer of olive oil. Get the olive oil hot because you're about to sear the flank steak.
4. Add steak and quickly sear for 3–4 minutes per side. Remove from the heat.
5. Remove steak from the pan and cut into bite-size pieces. Return cut-up steak to the skillet. Add tomato sauce and bring to a boil.
6. Line a baking tray with tortilla chips. Top with steak mixture. Sprinkle with cheese.
7. Bake nachos in oven for 15 minutes. If cheese starts browning too much, cover the nachos loosely with foil while they finish cooking.
8. *Make the chimichurri sauce:* Place all sauce ingredients in a blender. Blend until desired consistency is achieved, adding extra olive oil as needed to make sauce thinner.
9. When cheese has melted, remove nachos from the oven and serve with chimichurri sauce either on the side or directly on top of the nachos.

INGREDIENTS

For the nachos:

1 pound flank steak

3 tablespoons Brazilian seasonings (find a package at the store)

olive oil

1½ cups tomato sauce

lots and lots of tortilla chips

2 cups shredded cheese

For the chimichurri sauce:

1 cup olive oil

1 cup fresh parsley

½ cup fresh cilantro

1 tablespoon chopped or minced garlic

1 tablespoon oregano

1 teaspoon crushed red pepper flakes

dash of lemon juice

salt to taste

- Truthfully, I don't always get the meat marinated; I just season it and start cooking. So don't worry if you can't let it sit for a while.

SUMMER BBQS

Memorial Day marks the beginning of the summer season. In my family, my daddy, Hank, made the best BBQ in all of Sacramento (that's my story and I'm sticking to it). Memorial Day, July Fourth, and Labor Day were my daddy's big days.

What made my daddy's BBQ so good? I don't really know. He liked to experiment with different cooking techniques, but I don't know which ones worked better than others, 'cause his ribs were always on point. I can't think of a time when he didn't deliver the best, most tender ribs you've ever tasted.

And his sauces . . . Lawd have mercy! I saw so many bottles spread out on the kitchen counter, I'd lose count. He'd say, "Some of this one, some of this one . . . " Then he'd add some stuff to it. It was like watching a chemist perform a master experiment.

But I have got to tell y'all about my mama's fixings! Daddy only made the ribs. Everything else was Mama! She would make two sides. Yup, she only made two sides, and that's all we needed: baked beans and potato salad. Now I know you're thinking, "What kind of BBQ only has beans and potato salad?!"

Here's the key: you ain't never had my mama's beans and potato salad. Honey, let me tell you something. She would chop up vegetables like onions and bell peppers to add to the beans. And then she became her own master chemist! She would add some of whatever BBQ sauce concoction Daddy had created and some extra brown sugar, and then she topped it with bacon.

I'm going to tell on myself now. I used to sneak into the kitchen when she would take those beans out of the oven and try to fix my plate and get as much of the bacon as I could without anyone noticing. Sometimes she'd look back at the oven and say, "I thought I put more bacon in there." I didn't open my mouth! One of the few times in life I've been silent.

As for Mama's potato salad, that's a whole nother topic! Keep reading.

Aiden enjoying summer homemade ice cream

My secret bbq seasoning!

On the set of Good Day DC at Washington DC's Fox5

Chef Lorious' Homemade BBQ sauce

SMALL PLATES AND STARTERS-SUMMER BBQS

TANGY BROCCOLI SALAD

SERVES 2

This salad is like a blank canvas. You can substitute different meat, fruit, nuts . . . whatever you want! Instead of prosciutto (one of my favorites), you can use bacon or salami. In addition to dried cranberries, you can use raisins, dates, and/or figs. Of course, you can use whatever nut makes you sing—almonds, pecans, walnuts . . .

Directions

In a large bowl, combine all ingredients.

INGREDIENTS

- 1½ cups broccoli cut into bite sized pieces
- ½ cup mayonnaise
- 3 tablespoons apple cider vinegar
- 1 tablespoon sugar
- ½ cup prosciutto
- 2 tablespoons sliced almonds
- 2 tablespoons dried sweet cranberries

TIPS

★ The apple cider vinegar gives this salad its distinctive tang. I think I have a crush on apple cider vinegar and the kick it gives salads. If you're not a fan, add a little more sugar, or use a little less vinegar. This salad is your playground!

★ Broccoli florets will come small enough and require no additional cutting.

SHRIMP PO'BOY DIP

Serves 10

I think this is one of my favorite recipes because it was truly the result of my husband and I sitting down brainstorming ideas. A casual conversation resulted in a party appetizer that never lasts more than thirty minutes!

Directions

1. *Make the remoulade*: In a small bowl, combine all remoulade ingredients and mix together. Taste to see if you like the level of spice and seasoning, and adjust to your preference.
2. Preheat oven to 350 degrees F.
3. *Make the cream cheese dip base*: In a skillet, over medium heat, soften onions and garlic. When soft, remove from heat and add cream cheese. If the cream cheese doesn't melt, return to low heat and continue stirring. Stir in ¼ cup remoulade. Combine well and give it a taste. If you'd like a little more spicy kick, add some cayenne pepper. Bake in oven for 20 minutes, until cheese is bubbly.
4. *Prepare shrimp*: Season shrimp with creole seasoning. (This seasoning can be salty, so season the shrimp according to your preference.) Dip in flour mixture, then buttermilk mixture, then flour mixture.
5. *Fry shrimp*: In a sauté pan, heat peanut oil over medium-high heat. Test the oil by dropping a small drop of water into the pan. If the water sizzles, the oil is ready. Add shrimp in batches; do not overcrowd pan, or shrimp will not be crispy. Fry until golden brown,

INGREDIENTS

For the remoulade:

- ½ cup mayonnaise
- 1 tablespoon creole mustard
- 1 teaspoon parsley flakes
- 1 teaspoon lemon juice
- cayenne to taste
- hot sauce to taste

For the cream cheese dip base:

- 2 medium onions, chopped
- 2 tablespoons garlic, minced
- 1 (8-ounce) block cream cheese
- cayenne pepper to taste (optional)

For the fried shrimp:

- 2 pounds peeled and deveined shrimp, cut into bite-size pieces
- creole seasoning (buy some at your local grocery store)
- 1 cup flour mixed with 1 tablespoon creole seasoning
- 1 cup buttermilk mixed with 1 egg
- peanut oil, for frying
- hot sauce to taste

✶ TIPS

- ★ Don't feel pressured to make your own remoulade. You can easily do so, but sometimes you just don't have the time. You can purchase prepared remoulade at your local supermarket. If all else fails, mix your creole seasoning into plain mayonnaise, and keep tasting it until you're happy with the results.
- ★ Creole mustard isn't always easy to find. If you can't find it at your local supermarket, just use brown mustard and add Cajun or creole seasoning to it.
- ★ This dip works well with chips and with bread slices. Just be careful: I've never met a shrimp dip that lasted too long at a party!

approximately 3–5 minutes. Remove from oil and drain on a paper-towel-lined plate.

6. Toss shrimp in remaining remoulade sauce to coat.

7. After dip comes out of oven, place coated shrimp on top. Bake for another 7–10 minutes. Serve topped with hot sauce if you like.

SOUPS, CHOWDERS, AND STEWS

*N*othing warms the heart like soup, or so the saying goes. A warm bowl of soup can make the sun shine in your heart, especially on a cold winter day. But truth be told, you can enjoy soup any time of the year. I've been known to enjoy a big bowl of chowder in July.

The way I see it, there is a continuum from soup to chowder to stew that correlates with how filling the bowl is to your tummy. When I'm a little hungry, soup will do. But if I'm close to hangry, give me some stew!

BAKED POTATO AND BACON SOUP

Serves 6–8

*I*nitially, I considered not including this recipe because I figured we've all got enough potato soup recipes. But then I got to thinking, why not? It's a family favorite, and it welcomes autumn into our home like nothing else can.

INGREDIENTS

2 pounds bacon, cut into cubes

1 cup flour

5–6 cups chicken broth

3 pounds potatoes, baked, boiled, or microwaved until fork tender, peeled and cut into cubes

1 teaspoon nutmeg

½ teaspoon cayenne pepper (optional)

1½ cups heavy whipping cream

For garnish:

shredded cheese

chives

sour cream

bacon

Directions

1. In an 8-quart stockpot, cook bacon over medium heat until crisp. Set aside some of the cooked bacon to garnish the soup. Leave all of the bacon grease in the stockpot; you will use it to make a roux.

2. Add flour to the bacon in the stockpot and stir until absorbed by the bacon grease. Add chicken broth and bring to a boil. Stir constantly until the mixture begins to thicken.

3. Add cooked potatoes, nutmeg, and cayenne (if using). Stir well to combine. Add the heavy whipping cream and bring to a boil.

4. Let the soup simmer for about 10 minutes until all flavors are well combined. Taste to be sure it's the way you want it.

5. Garnish with sour cream, cheese, bacon pieces, chives—whatever you like on your baked potato.

TIPS

★ For a thicker soup, add an extra ¼ cup of flour at a time until desired thickness is achieved. Dissolve the flour in ⅓ cup of water or broth so it doesn't get lumpy in the soup.

★ Don't worry about pureeing or mashing the potatoes. As the soup simmers, they will melt into the liquid. Whatever pieces don't fully dissolve will be delicious chunks of soft potatoes in your soup.

CORN, BACON, AND POTATO CHOWDER

SERVES 6–8

When I make a pot of soup, I have a hard time knowing when to stop adding stuff. I go in the refrigerator and think, "Oh, that would be perfect!" That's how this soup ended being corn, bacon, and potato. I just kept adding things. So feel free to add some more goodies when you make it too. The more the merrier!

INGREDIENTS

- 1 pound bacon, cut into cubes
- 2 yellow onions, chopped
- 2 jalapeños, chopped
- 1 poblano pepper, chopped
- 1 cup flour
- 8 cups chicken broth
- 6 red potatoes, cubed
- 6 cups corn, fresh or frozen
- 2 cups heavy whipping cream (or half-and-half)
- 1 cup shredded cheddar cheese, plus more for garnish
- 1 tablespoon chopped cilantro
- 1 teaspoon cayenne (optional)
- 2 teaspoons salt

Directions

1. In an 8-quart stockpot, cook bacon over medium heat until crisp.
2. Add onions, jalapeños, and poblano to the bacon in the stockpot. Cook until soft.
3. Add flour to the stockpot and stir until absorbed by the bacon grease. Add chicken broth and bring to a boil. Stir constantly until the mixture begins to thicken.
4. Add potatoes and cook in the broth mixture until you can stick a fork through them. Add corn and cream. Stir to combine well. Add shredded cheese and stir to allow cheese to melt. Add cilantro, cayenne (if using), and salt. Stir all ingredients together and bring to a boil.
5. Reduce heat to medium low and simmer for 20–30 minutes as soup thickens. Stir frequently to keep soup from sticking to the bottom of the pot.
6. Garnish soup with reserved bacon and additional shredded cheese.

TIPS

★ Set aside some of the cooked bacon to garnish the soup.
★ Leave all of the bacon grease in the stockpot; you will use it to make a roux.
★ Potatoes shouldn't be mushy like mashed potatoes but should be soft enough for a fork or toothpick to go completely through them. This should take about 10 minutes.

SAUSAGE TORTELLINI SOUP WITH SPINACH

Serves 6–8

INGREDIENTS

- 2 cups cheese tortellini
- olive oil, for sautéing
- 1 tablespoon garlic, minced or chopped
- 1 yellow onion, chopped
- 1 green bell pepper, chopped
- 1 cup sliced mushrooms
- 1 pound mild ground sausage
- 1 pound sweet ground sausage
- 1 cup all-purpose flour
- 3 tablespoons basil
- 2 tablespoons parsley
- 1 tablespoon oregano
- 8 cups chicken broth
- 3–4 cups spinach
- salt, pepper, and red pepper flakes to taste
- shredded italian cheese, for garnish

This is the kind of soup that makes my family sing. There's something about having pasta and sausage in the same warm pot that is just magical. Now here's my mom tip: the kiddos don't even notice the spinach in there! It's a great way to sneak some veggies into them. I also use kale sometimes, because why not? The more greens the better.

Directions

1. In a medium pot, bring water to a boil. Add tortellini and cook for 3–4 minutes until they begin to soften. (They should not be completely done, just beginning to soften.) Remove tortellini from water so they don't continue cooking and set aside.

2. In an 8-quart stockpot, heat olive oil over medium-high heat. (You just need enough olive oil to cover the bottom of the pan. The sausage will render the fat needed to make the roux for the soup.) Add garlic, onion, bell pepper, and mushrooms and sauté until soft.

3. Add all of the sausage to the stockpot and continue cooking until sausage is fully cooked. Break up sausage as it cooks.

4. When sausage is done cooking, add the flour and stir until flour is absorbed by the oil and sausage grease rendered in the pot.

5. Add basil, parsley, and oregano to the stockpot. Combine well.
6. Add chicken broth and bring to a boil. Stir constantly until the mixture begins to thicken.
7. Add the spinach slowly (one handful at a time), allowing the broth to reduce the spinach as you continue adding it.
8. After all spinach is added and has cooked down, add the cooked tortellini. Bring to a boil; reduce heat to medium low and simmer until desired thickness is achieved, about 20 minutes.
9. Garnish with shredded cheese.

SPICY SEAFOOD, CHICKEN, AND SAUSAGE STEW

SERVES 8–10

*T*o some, this is a form of gumbo. To some, it's a form of étouffée. To some, it's a spicy seafood stew. I am always cautious when I say it's *gumbo* because our friends in the Crescent City have a special patent on gumbo, and I would hate to upset them! So, in true Calibama style, I'll just call it my creation, my adaptation, my spicy seafood stew. You can call yours whatever you like!

INGREDIENTS

- olive oil, for sautéing
- 1 yellow onion, chopped
- 1 green bell pepper, chopped
- 4 cloves garlic, minced or chopped
- 1 pound spicy Cajun andouille sausage, cut into bite-size pieces
- 1 pound kielbasa sausage, cut into bite-size pieces
- 1 cup vegetable oil
- 1 cup all-purpose flour
- 6 cups chicken broth
- 1 (28-ounce) can crushed or diced tomatoes
- 2 teaspoons thyme to taste
- 2 teaspoons crushed red pepper flakes
- ½ cup okra (optional)
- 1 pound chicken breast, cut into bite-size pieces
- 1 pound shrimp, peeled and deveined
- 2 cups corn, fresh or frozen
- 1 pound crabmeat, cut into bite-size pieces
- salt and pepper

Directions

1. In a large stockpot, heat 1–2 tablespoons of olive oil over medium-high heat. Add onion, bell pepper, and garlic; cook until fragrant. (The vegetables shouldn't be mushy soft; they should just be starting to soften.)
2. Add the andouille and kielbasa to the stockpot. Cook until onion becomes translucent. Remove sausage and veggies from pot and set aside.
3. In the same stockpot, combine vegetable oil and flour. Whisk together and cook until flour smells toasty but not burnt. For a dark roux, continue cooking and stirring
4. Slowly pour chicken broth into roux. Stir constantly until mixture is completely combined.
5. Return sausage and veggies to stockpot. Combine well.
6. Add the tomatoes, thyme, and red pepper flakes. If using okra, add now. Combine well.

7. Bring to a boil, then lower heat to medium low and cook, uncovered, for about 1 hour.

8. Fill a separate pot with water and bring to a boil for poaching the chicken and shrimp. First, poach the chicken in the boiling water until the outside of the meat begins to turn opaque white, about 4 minutes. Remove with a slotted spoon and set aside to add to the stockpot. Next, poach the shrimp in the boiling water until the outside of the shrimp begins to turn opaque white, 2–3 minutes. Remove with a slotted spoon and set aside to add to the stockpot. (The chicken and shrimp don't need to be completely cooked; they just need to start cooking and have the outside turn white. They will finish cooking in the stockpot with the rest of the ingredients.)

9. Add the poached chicken to the stockpot. Then add the corn and cook all together for about 30 minutes.

10. Add the poached shrimp and the crabmeat to the stockpot. Stir well to combine everything in pot. Add salt and pepper to taste.

11. Allow stew to simmer for 30–45 minutes more to allow flavors to blend.

12. Serve alone or with rice and corn bread.

BEEF STEW

Serves 8–10

Crock-Pot meals are essential to every household. This stew can also be made in the Instant Pot. I personally love my Instant Pot! But I can't let go of my good ol' Crock-Pot; it reminds me of my grandma. Wherever you cook this, enjoy the warm memories it's sure to stir up.

Directions

1. Cover entire pot roast with olive oil and season both sides well with salt, garlic powder, onion powder, and pepper. Place directly in Crock-Pot with no additional liquid and cook on high for two hours.
2. Add vegetables, herbs, broth, and wine. Continue cooking on high for two more hours.
3. Remove meat from Crock-Pot. Pull the meat apart or cut the meat and return it to the pot.
4. Continue cooking until vegetables are soft, 1–2 hours more.

INGREDIENTS

1½ pounds beef pot roast

1 tablespoon olive oil

1 tablespoon salt

2 teaspoons garlic powder

2 teaspoons onion powder

2 tablespoons pepper

2 yellow onions, chopped

1 cup baby carrots

1 cup baby bella mushrooms, sliced

6 medium red potatoes, diced

2 tablespoons basil

2 tablespoons parsley

3 cups beef broth

2 cups red cooking wine

CALIBAMA CHILI

Serves 8–10

*E*verybody's chili has a special secret ingredient, and mine is no exception. What makes Calibama Chili unique, in my opinion, is not just my special ingredient but also the excluded items: beans! My family doesn't particularly like beans in their chili, so I've adapted my recipe not to include them. Be aware, this is award-winning chili, so however you choose to modify it, it will still be the best ever!

INGREDIENTS

- 2–3 tablespoons olive oil
- 1 large yellow onion, chopped
- 1 large green bell pepper, chopped
- 3 tablespoons garlic, minced
- 2 pounds ground beef
- 1 pound hot ground sausage
- 1 pound mild ground sausage
- ¾ cup all-purpose flour
- ¾ cup cooking oil (vegetable or canola)
- ⅔ cup chili powder
- 6 tablespoons cumin
- 3 tablespoons chipotle pepper
- 3 tablespoons oregano
- 2 (15-ounce) cans red kidney beans (optional)
- 2 cups beef broth
- 2 cups stout beer
- 2 (15-ounce) cans fire-roasted tomatoes
- 1 teaspoon cayenne pepper (optional)
- sour cream, for topping
- shredded cheese, for topping

Directions

1. In an 8-quart stockpot, heat olive oil over medium heat. Add onion, bell pepper, and garlic; cook until softened.
2. When the onion begins to look translucent, add ground beef and sausage. Cook together until meat is done. Remove from pot and set aside. Do not drain the fat.
3. In the same stockpot, combine flour and cooking oil. Stir constantly to avoid sticking and clumping. Cook until mixture begins to bubble slightly and the flour is absorbed into the oil. Do not bring to a boil.
4. Add chili powder, cumin, chipotle pepper, and oregano. Stir well to combine.
5. Add meat (including the fat), vegetables, and beans (if using beans) to the seasoned roux. Stir and combine well.
6. Add beef broth and beer. Stir well and bring everything to a boil. Let simmer, stirring occasionally, for 45 minutes (ideally).

7. Add tomatoes. Combine well and simmer on low for another 30–45 minutes.

8. Finally, add cayenne pepper if desired. Combine all and simmer until ready to eat.

9. Serve chili topped with sour cream, cheese, and anything else that makes chili good to you.

CHICKEN POT PIE

SERVES 6

I don't think chicken pot pie is really a soup, chowder, or stew. But since the inside is so thick and full of delicious and filling ingredients, I decided it belonged here. And it tastes amazing on cold-weather days!

Directions

1. Preheat oven to 375 degrees F.
2. In a large skillet, heat olive oil over medium heat. Add carrots, green beans, and onion and cook until they begin to soften, about 3 minutes.
3. Add garlic, thyme, and basil. Continue cooking until soft, 3–4 minutes more.
4. Add chicken and combine all items in the skillet very well.
5. Sprinkle in flour and stir to coat well. Slowly pour in chicken broth, stirring as you pour. Bring to a boil, and sauce will begin to thicken. The mixture should be somewhat loose, not overly thick. If the mixture is too thick, it will be dry after baking.
6. Place one piecrust on the bottom of a deep-dish pie plate. Pour the chicken mixture into the piecrust. Top the mixture with the other piecrust.
7. Seal the edges and brush with the egg wash. Cut small slits into the top to allow steam to escape while baking.
8. Place pie on a baking sheet and bake until golden brown, 35–40 minutes.
9. Remove from oven and allow to rest for about 10 minutes before serving.

INGREDIENTS

- 2–3 tablespoons olive oil
- ½ cup sliced carrots
- ½ cup cut green beans (cut small)
- ½ cup diced onion
- 1 teaspoon garlic, minced
- 1 tablespoon dried thyme
- 1 tablespoon dried basil
- 1½ pounds boneless, skinless chicken breasts or thighs, cooked and cut into bite-size pieces
- 2–3 tablespoons all-purpose flour
- 1 cup chicken broth
- ¾ cup heavy whipping cream
- 2 (9-inch) piecrusts (store-bought or Lori's No-Mess Perfect Piecrust, page 229)
- 1 egg, lightly beaten with 2 tablespoons water
- salt and pepper, to taste

GUINNESS SHEPHERD'S STEW

This is my version of shepherd's pie. I don't know why, but I've never been a fan of the stuff. So I created my own version that makes me sing. Don't make it thin; make sure it's thick and filling. When you put a big scoop of mashed potatoes on top, I hear you singing too!

Directions

1. In an 8-quart stockpot, heat olive oil over medium heat. Add carrots, mushrooms, cabbage, onions, and garlic and cook until softened. Remove from pot and set aside.

2. Season chuck roast with garlic powder, onion powder, thyme, salt, and pepper. Coat with flour.

3. Add the seasoned meat to the stockpot and cook until slightly browned. Do not cook meat completely.

4. Return vegetables to stockpot and cook until cabbage begins to wilt. Stir frequently so meat does not overcook and nothing sticks to bottom of pot.

5. Pour in Guinness and beef broth and bring to a boil.

6. To thicken soup, add additional flour, ¼ cup at a time. Dissolve additional flour in ⅓ cup of water or broth before adding to the soup pot.

7. While stew is thickening, make mashed potatoes. Serve on top of stew.

Serves 6–8

INGREDIENTS

2 tablespoons olive oil
1 cup baby carrots
1 cup mushrooms
1 cup cut-up cabbage
2 large yellow onions, chopped
3 garlic cloves, chopped or minced
½ pound beef chuck roast, cubed
3 tablespoons garlic powder
3 tablespoons onion powder
1 tablespoon thyme
salt and pepper
½ cup flour
1 large can Guinness beer
5 cups beef broth
mashed potatoes, for topping

TIPS

★ I typically use traditional Guinness stout for this recipe. It can also be made with Guinness's lighter cousin, Boddingtons Pub Ale. Both of these stouts have a smooth, rich flavor that works wonderfully with the beef in this recipe.

★ To make mashed potatoes, boil the potatoes in salty water until a skewer can easily go through. Peel the potatoes when done cooking and mash. Add butter and milk to the taste and consistency desired. In this recipe, I like to leave the potatoes a little chunky. That way, they absorb a lot of the stew juice.

TURKEY TORTILLA SOUP

Serves 6–8

I generally am not a big fan of ground turkey meat, but I really enjoy it in this soup. You can substitute shredded chicken, ground chicken, or even ground beef. To make it extra spicy, use hot salsa, or just add some plain old hot sauce!

INGREDIENTS

- 2 tablespoons olive oil
- 1 yellow onion, chopped
- 3 cloves garlic, chopped
- 1 pound lean ground turkey meat
- 3 tablespoons cumin
- 3 tablespoons cilantro
- 2 tablespoons chili powder
- 2 tablespoons garlic powder
- 1 teaspoon salt
- 1 (24-ounce) jar salsa
- 6½–8 cups chicken broth
- ½ cup all-purpose flour, plus more for thickening
- 1 cup shredded cheese, plus more for garnish
- tortilla chips

Directions

1. In a large 8-quart stockpot, heat oil over medium heat. Add onion and garlic and cook until softened.
2. Add ground turkey, cumin, cilantro, chili powder, garlic powder, and salt. Continue cooking until the turkey meat is done. Combine well.
3. Add salsa and combine well.
4. Pour in 6 cups chicken broth. Stir well.
5. Whisk the ½ cup flour into ½ cup of remaining chicken broth. Whisk until smooth and add to pot of cooking soup.
6. Stir in shredded cheese. Bring to a boil, then reduce heat to medium and simmer for 20–30 minutes.
7. To thicken soup, add additional flour ¼ cup at a time, dissolving in ⅓ cup water or broth before adding to the pot. (Note: This is in addition to the flour used in step 3. It is an optional step if you want your soup to be thicker.)
8. Serve with tortilla chips and extra shredded cheese.

MAIN COURSES

Can I be honest? I don't think I could be a vegetarian. I can handle the occasional "meatless Monday," but I'm a real carnivore. I love a good steak, and I can't turn down thick-cut bacon. So, dare I say, this could be my favorite section of the whole cookbook. I'm also quite a fan of spicy foods, so I can easily be talked into any spicy chicken or pasta dish. I trust that within these next pages, you can find a savory dish to satisfy your inner meat-eater.

ROSEMARY SEARED CHICKEN THIGHS

This is one of my go-to quick meals. It doesn't take long to make, and the cast-iron skillet makes all the difference in the world. It's fast and elegant—sounds like a win-win to me.

Directions

1. Preheat oven to 400 degrees F.
2. In a cast-iron skillet, heat olive oil over medium heat. Add onion and garlic and cook until just soft. Remove with a slotted spoon and set aside, leaving oil in skillet.
3. Season chicken thighs with salt and pepper. Place in the hot olive oil remaining in the skillet, skin-side down. Leave skin-side down until skin begins to pull away from the bottom of the skillet. Turn chicken over and cook for an additional 2–3 minutes. Remove from skillet and set aside.
4. Reduce heat. Add butter and rosemary to skillet. When butter melts, add white wine to deglaze pan.
5. Return chicken to skillet, skin-side up. Return onion and garlic to skillet. Cook 5–7 minutes.
6. Place skillet in oven and cook for approximately 20 minutes until chicken is done. (To check if the chicken is done, stick a knife or fork into the thickest part of the chicken. If the juices run clear, it's done.)
7. Remove from oven and serve.

Serves 4

INGREDIENTS

4 tablespoons olive oil
1 yellow onion, sliced
2 cloves garlic, minced
4 chicken thighs (with skin on)
salt and pepper
½ cup unsalted butter, softened
2 tablespoons chopped fresh rosemary
1 cup dry white wine
rosemary sprigs

TIP

★ To get crispy seared chicken, you need two things: hot oil and chicken skin. Season the meat with salt and pepper only, at least initially. Adding herbs directly to the meat will cause them to burn in the hot oil. So first sear the meat with salt and pepper, then add your herbs and continue cooking.

LORIOUS CHICKEN AND WAFFLES

Serves 6–8

*T*his is my signature dish. When I schedule cooking demos, this is typically what I make. One taste, and you're a fan for life! I serve it with my specialty Sriracha Maple Syrup, but to taste that, you'll have to come to a cooking demo.

Directions

1. Season chicken with seasoning mix. Be sure all pieces are thoroughly coated. (Seriously, don't skimp on the seasoning. You don't want your chicken to be boring. Show it some love, and just when you think you're done seasoning the chicken, season it again!)

2. In a medium bowl, combine buttermilk, egg, and hot sauce. Add chicken and let sit for 30 minutes or more. (If you can't wait, that's okay. The chicken will still be good even if it doesn't marinate in the buttermilk.)

3. In another medium bowl, combine ingredients for seasoned flour.

4. In a skillet, heat oil to about 350 degrees (I recommend peanut oil).

5. Dredge each piece of chicken in seasoned flour. Add to skillet and fry 7–10 minutes, depending on thickness.

6. Prepare the waffles—or, to save time, heat up store-bought prepared waffles.

7. Serve with maple syrup.

INGREDIENTS

2 pounds chicken breast tenders

seasoning mix: combine 1 tablespoon each of salt, seasoned pepper, chili powder, Cajun seasoning, and cayenne pepper

2 cups buttermilk

1 egg

½ cup hot sauce

vegetable oil, for frying

waffles or store-bought waffles (see tip in Chocolate Waffles recipe, page 221)

maple syrup, for serving

For the seasoned flour:

1 cup all-purpose flour

1 teaspoon salt

1 tablespoon chili powder

2 tablespoons Cajun seasoning

1 teaspoon seasoned pepper

1 tablespoon cayenne

DIP DINNERS

So by now, you know I'm still a church girl at heart. And I make no apologies for it. I love being a church girl. There's something about the pure, honest naiveté that comes from being raised in a sheltered environment. You can't stay in the shelter your whole life, but it is fun to reflect on how differently the world operates when you step outside.

Anyway, when I think about my church upbringing as it relates to food, my thoughts always go back to the annex. Now I know you're thinking, "What is the annex?" Our church was a real church building on the corner of Fig and Harris Streets in a residential community. Next to our church was a house that our church bought and used as a fellowship hall. We called it the annex. We were always in church all day on Sundays. The morning started at nine thirty with Sunday school, then a noon service, a seven thirty evening service, and quite frequently a special afternoon service at three or four. Well, if you're going to be out all day, you gotta eat.

We started with a snack between Sunday school and morning service. Our definition of a snack was fried chicken and lemon cake. Yes: at eleven thirty in the morning, we ate fried chicken thighs, legs, and wings with lemon cake. (And we wonder why heart disease and diabetes are so prevalent!) That could get you through the service. You just had to keep moving so you didn't fall asleep.

After service was when the real eating took place. We would have what we called "dip dinners." This was an ongoing fund-raiser. A *dip* was a serving, and each dip cost fifty cents. Everything would be laid out buffet-style, and you went down the line and fixed your plate. At the end of the line, someone would tally up your total. Then you could sit down and eat as much as you wanted. Go back for seconds, thirds, even fourths—just make sure someone writes down how many dips you took.

I know this sounds strange and funny, but I promise you, it's not made up. We paid for a church building, bought choir robes, and took youth trips, all from dip dinners.

All of the ladies in the church would bring one dish to the dinner on Sundays. As you can imagine, it was an absolute feast. In the spirit of honesty, everybody couldn't cook, and some folks should have kept their dishes at home. But you knew who made what, and some dishes were sacred. Macaroni and cheese couldn't be made by just anybody. Same with collard greens, potato salad, and pound cake. I didn't realize I was a li'l foodie at the time, because I could taste the difference in how the chicken was seasoned, how moist the cakes were, and how salty the greens were. It didn't bother me; I could just recognize the taste. I knew my Grandmama's sweet potato pie anywhere. I could pick it out of a lineup! And I know Mrs. C's fried chicken too.

Those were the good ol' days: church, chicken, and family.

GARLIC CREAM CHICKEN

Serves 6

This is one of the best mishaps I've ever had in the kitchen. It was a Saturday night, and I just couldn't bring myself to order another pizza. So I got creative, and the next thing I knew, a new family classic was born. Sometimes the best things are born out of frustration and necessity.

Directions

1. Coat the bottom of a skillet with olive oil. Heat the oil over medium heat while you prepare the chicken.
2. Coat chicken with olive oil and then salt, pepper, onion powder, garlic powder, basil leaves, thyme leaves, and oregano.
3. Place seasoned chicken in skillet with the hot oil. Cook until brown on the outside but not completely done. Remove from skillet and set aside.
4. Add butter, garlic, and onion to skillet and cook over medium heat until the vegetables begin to soften.
5. In a medium bowl, combine cream, chicken broth, and flour. Whisk until smooth.
6. Pour cream mixture into skillet with garlic and onion and continue cooking until sauce begins to boil and thicken. Be sure to continue stirring.
7. Reduce heat to medium, return chicken thighs to the skillet, and allow all to cook together for 10–15 minutes, until chicken is completely done.

INGREDIENTS

extra virgin olive oil, to coat the chicken and the bottom of the skillet

8–10 boneless chicken thighs

1 teaspoon salt

1 teaspoon pepper

1 tablespoon onion powder

1 tablespoon garlic powder

1 teaspoon chopped basil leaves (fresh or dried)

1 teaspoon thyme leaves (fresh or dried)

1 teaspoon chopped oregano (fresh or dried)

½ cup butter (1 stick)

3 tablespoons garlic, minced

1 medium yellow onion, sliced thinly

2 cups cream (milk, half and half, or heavy cream)

1 cup chicken broth

¾ cup flour

TIP

★ If you use chicken with bones, it will take longer to cook (about twenty minutes more). Boneless meat cooks quicker, but bone-in meat is juicier. So you gotta decide how you want to do it!

GARLIC AND BROWN SUGAR PORK TENDERLOIN

*T*his is one of my fail-proof weekday dinners. The garlic and brown sugar make for an amazing flavor combination. Pork tenderloin is like a hidden gem in the meat aisle. It cooks relatively quickly (thirty minutes or so), and it receives flavors very well. When you can get dinner on the table, gourmet quality, and amazing flavors in under an hour, score one for Mom!

Directions

1. Preheat oven to 400 degrees F.
2. Coat bottom of an ovenproof skillet with olive oil and heat over medium-high heat.
3. In a large bowl, combine salt, pepper, brown sugar, and olive oil. Add pork tenderloin and coat completely with the mixture.
4. Place coated pork in skillet with hot olive oil and sear on all sides for 5–7 minutes. Do not cook it completely; just get the outside golden brown. Be sure to turn the pork frequently so all sides can get evenly browned. Remove pork from pan and set aside.
5. *Make the sauce:* Melt butter in same skillet. Add brown sugar, garlic, parsley, and salt. Bring to a boil and add thyme sprigs and sage leaves.
6. Return pork to skillet with sauce. Place a lid on skillet and bake for 20 minutes.
7. Remove pork from oven and let rest 5–7 minutes before slicing. Top with the sauce from the pan.

Serves 6

INGREDIENTS

For the pork tenderloin:

- olive oil, for coating skillet and pork
- 1 teaspoon salt
- 1 teaspoon pepper
- 1 tablespoon brown sugar
- 2 pounds pork tenderloin

For the sauce:

- 1 cup butter (2 sticks)
- 2 tablespoons brown sugar
- 5 cloves garlic, chopped
- 2 tablespoons chopped parsley
- 1 teaspoon salt
- 1 bunch thyme sprigs
- 4–5 fresh sage leaves

TIPS

★ Be sure to let the tenderloin rest when you remove it from the oven. The resting time is important to let the juices stay inside the meat. If you cut it too soon, the juices will run out, and you'll miss out on the goodness that you just baked into it.

★ If you don't have an ovenproof skillet to cook the entire dish in, transfer the pork and sauce to a roasting pan or baking dish before putting it in the oven.

HEARTY CHICKEN PICCATA

*T*his was one of my mom's go-to meals. She would make this when she needed to get dinner on the table quickly. In recreating one of my childhood favorites, I decided to thicken up the sauce to give it a little bit more of the South.

Directions

1. Coat skillet with olive oil and heat over medium heat.
2. Set aside 1 teaspoon garlic powder, 1 teaspoon onion powder, 1 teaspoon salt, and ½ teaspoon black pepper. Use remainder to season chicken breasts.
3. In a medium bowl, combine reserved seasonings with the flour to create a seasoned coating.
4. Dredge chicken in eggs and then in seasoned flour. Place in hot olive oil in skillet and cook until coating begins to brown and chicken is about 90 percent done.
5. Remove chicken and set aside. Deglaze the pan by slowly pouring in chicken broth and lemon juice. Bring liquid to a boil and return chicken to pan.
6. Add capers, reduce heat to medium, and allow chicken to finish cooking while absorbing the sauce into the coating of the chicken.

Serves 6

INGREDIENTS

extra virgin olive oil

1 tablespoon garlic powder, divided

1 tablespoon onion powder, divided

2 teaspoons salt, divided

1 teaspoon black pepper, divided

1 pound chicken breasts, boneless and skinless

1 cup all-purpose flour

2 eggs, lightly beaten

2 cups chicken broth

½ cup lemon juice

2 tablespoons capers

★ For a slightly different flavor profile, use dry white wine instead of chicken broth. You'll unlock a whole new dimension.

BEEF AND SAUSAGE MEATLOAF

Some foods are the very definition of comfort food. Meatloaf is one of those foods. Instead of a full meatloaf mix, I like to just use ground beef and sausage. Also, the addition of parmesan cheese makes this definitely not your mama's meatloaf! Calibama cooking is all about putting your own spin on your favorite classics.

Directions

1. Preheat oven to 350 degrees F.
2. In a large skillet, heat enough olive oil to cover the skillet over medium-high heat until hot. Add the garlic and onions and cook until soft.
3. Remove skillet from heat and add salt, pepper, and Worcestershire sauce. Set aside.
4. In a large bowl, gently fold the ground beef and sausage into each other, being careful not to overmix the ingredients.
5. Add the onion mixture, bread crumbs, eggs, and parmesan. Mix with your hands, but don't overwork it. Overmixing will make the meatloaf too dense.
6. Form the meat mixture into two loaves on a well-sprayed baking rack. Cover with sauce (see below) and sprinkle brown sugar on top.
7. Bake at 350 degrees for 25 minutes. Take out of oven and baste again with sauce and sprinkle additional brown sugar on top.

MAKES 2 MEATLOAVES

INGREDIENTS

3 tablespoons minced garlic

3 cups chopped yellow onions

1 teaspoon salt

1 teaspoon seasoned pepper

3 tablespoons Worcestershire sauce

2 pounds ground beef

½ pound ground italian sausage

¾ cup bread crumbs

2 eggs, lightly beaten

1½ cups parmesan cheese, shredded or grated

1 tablespoon Dijon mustard

2 tablespoons parsley

For the sauce:

3 cups ketchup

3 tablespoons brown sugar

dash Worcestershire sauce

dash Dijon mustard

TIPS

★ Be sure to spray the baking sheet well so the meatloaves don't stick.

★ The sausage helps accentuate the flavor of the beef in a way that is indescribable.

8. Return to oven and continue baking for 20–25 more minutes, until meat reaches an internal temperature of 165 degrees.

9. Combine all sauce ingredients. Taste to see if you like it! Serve the sauce over the meatloaf.

LORI'S MEATY MARINARA SAUCE

*T*his is my signature red pasta sauce. I love to make it in big batches because it freezes so well. This sauce works in lasagna, spaghetti, and any type of red-sauce-friendly dish. Don't be surprised if it doesn't make it to the freezer. I've seen my family eat the sauce all by itself!

Directions

1. In an 8-quart stockpot, heat olive oil over medium heat until hot. Add onion, bell pepper, and garlic and sauté until soft. Be careful not to burn the garlic.
2. Add the garlic powder, oregano, and basil and combine well.
3. After approximately 5 minutes, add mushrooms. Cook until mushrooms begin to soften.
4. When mushrooms are soft, add ground beef and sausage. Combine the meat and vegetables well and continue cooking.
5. When meat is cooked, add tomato sauce and bring to a boil.
6. Add tomatoes and cooking wine. Stir well. Taste and add additional seasonings if necessary. Add sugar (to reduce the acidity of the tomatoes) and let the sauce simmer 30 minutes or more to allow all the flavors to come together.

Makes 1 large pot

INGREDIENTS

2–3 tablespoons extra virgin olive oil, for cooking

1 yellow onion, diced

1 green bell pepper, diced

2 garlic cloves, minced

¼ cup garlic powder

3 tablespoons oregano

2 tablespoons basil

1 cup baby portobello mushrooms

2 pounds ground beef

2 pounds ground pork sausage

3 (29-ounce) cans tomato sauce

3 (15-ounce) cans diced tomatoes, with their juice

1 cup red cooking wine (see note below)

2 tablespoons white sugar

TIP

★ If you don't want to use cooking wine, you can substitute beef broth. The sauce will still taste delicious.

BEEF STROGANOFF

I'll never forget the first time I made this. I was telling my mom about my plan to make beef stroganoff for dinner, and I mentioned that I'd never had it but a lot of people liked it. She promptly told me that she made it frequently when I was a little girl. I insisted that she had to be mistaken because I didn't ever remember it. Then I made it, and when I tasted it I looked at her and said, "That's what that was? You made this a lot. I didn't know it was beef stroganoff!"

Directions

1. In a large skillet, heat olive oil over medium heat.
2. Meanwhile, season pot roast with salt and pepper to taste. When oil is hot, add roast to skillet over medium-high heat and quickly sear each side. Do not overcrowd the pan. Turn the meat over to sear both sides. Remove meat and set aside. Reduce heat to medium.
3. In the same skillet, combine garlic, onion, and mushrooms. Cook over medium heat until soft.
4. In a medium bowl, whisk together 1 cup beef broth and ½ cup flour. Add the remaining 3 cups beef broth to the skillet. Once the broth and veggies in the skillet are boiling, add the broth with the dissolved flour.
5. Return seared beef cubes to the. Boil gently until meat is done, 5–7 minutes.
6. Continue gently boiling and add the sour cream. Stir well to dissolve.
7. Serve beef mixture over noodles.

SERVES 6

INGREDIENTS

olive oil, for searing

2 pounds beef pot roast, cut into cubes

salt and pepper to taste

2 tablespoons minced garlic

1 yellow onion

2 cups sliced mushrooms

4 cups beef broth, divided

1 cup cooking sherry

½–1 cup flour

1 cup sour cream

1 (12-ounce) bag egg noodles, cooked according to package directions

★ This meal can go from stovetop to table in thirty minutes. It's one of those great dishes to have in your back pocket when you need to get dinner on the table but don't have a lot of time. Add a quick side salad, and you've got a complete meal.

CRAB-TOPPED FILET MIGNON

SERVES 2

I love a good steak as much as the next gal, and there's nothing like a good steak prepared at home. My husband and I enjoy eating out, and we almost always end up at a steakhouse. But I gotta be honest here: we have fallen in love with making our own steaks at home. This crab topping is phenomenal, and even better, you can replace it with anything you fancy. Let your imagination run wild!

Directions

Cook the filets:

1. Preheat oven to 450 degrees F.
2. In an oven-safe skillet, heat the butter or olive oil over medium-high heat.
3. Rinse filets and pat dry. Cover all sides generously with steak seasoning.
4. Place the seasoned filets in the hot skillet. Sear for 2–3 minutes per side and around the edges.
5. Place the skillet with the steaks in the preheated oven for 5–8 minutes, until desired doneness is achieved.

For the topping:

1. Meanwhile, in a separate skillet, heat butter or olive oil over medium heat. Add asparagus and mushrooms and sauté until softened.
2. Add minced garlic and then crabmeat; continue cooking until veggies are tender and crabmeat is

INGREDIENTS

For the filet mignon:

- butter or olive oil, for sautéing
- 2 filet mignon (single-serving-size) steaks
- steak seasoning

For the topping:

- butter or olive oil, for sautéing
- 1 bunch asparagus
- 1 cup sliced mushrooms
- 1 tablespoon garlic, minced or chopped
- 1 cup jumbo lump crabmeat
- salt and pepper to taste

For the béarnaise sauce:

- ¼ cup white wine vinegar
- ¼ cup dry white wine (I recommend sauvignon blanc)
- 1 small shallot, minced
- 2 tablespoons chopped tarragon leaves
- 3 egg yolks
- 2–4 sticks unsalted butter, melted
- salt and pepper to taste

thoroughly warmed. Season with salt and pepper to taste. (A little steak seasoning is also a nice touch!)

For the béarnaise sauce:

1. In a medium saucepan over medium heat, combine the vinegar, wine, shallot, and tarragon and bring to a boil. Allow to simmer for 3–5 minutes. Remove from heat.
2. In a blender (or with a whisk), combine the egg yolks until they come together and are smooth. Slowly add to the wine mixture and blend. (Don't dump the egg yolks in all at once, because the heat from the wine mixture can cook the eggs. Slowly add the egg yolks and continue stirring the entire time.)
3. Once the egg yolks and wine mixture have come together, slowly pour in melted butter. Continue blending until well combined and creamy, using a whisk, hand immersion blender, or the kitchen blender you used for the egg yolks initially. (Either blender will give you the best results, but if you don't have one, use a whisk.)
4. Add salt and pepper to taste.

Assemble and serve:

1. Add steaks to plates and top with crabmeat. Place asparagus and mushrooms on the side. Spoon warm béarnaise sauce over the entire dish.

THE LOVE OF MY LIFE

Every girl wants to fall in love. Every girl wants to be swept off her feet. Every girl wants to feel like she is the most beautiful and important person in the world to someone. Not many of us find the type of unconditional love that our hearts yearn for. I have been blessed beyond measure because I have that type of love in my life—now.

I have made the same mistakes in love that most women have. I've fallen in love too early, fallen in love with the wrong guy, stayed too long . . . the story goes on and on. But one of the things I'm most thankful for is my faith and the tremendous blessings that I have been given by my heavenly Father. Don't worry, this isn't about to become a religious book—but everybody believes in something.

The beautiful thing about faith is that it guides your life and directs your heart even if you're unaware that it's happening. The thing(s) you believe in will be the thing(s) that drive your decision making. Those same beliefs and decisions will position you for each stage of your life. In the deepest places of my heart and soul, I believe in the eternal, everlasting, and unconditional love of Father God. That is the key belief that drives my decision making.

What does that have to do with my life's love story? Good question!

Although I've had my heart broken, my belief in Father God's love allowed my heart to remain open to receive and experience the type of unconditional love we all want. That shared faith and belief system is what attracted my husband and me to each other.

Often in our immaturity, we mistake compatibility with love. Inexperience can make it difficult to tell the difference between separate interests and separate belief systems. My own immaturity at times has caused me to make those misjudgments. That's where faith and grace come in.

I have been blessed to experience true love with my wonderful husband. He loves me more than words can describe, and I love him more than I can explain. From that unconditional and undying love, we have both been able to grow and discover our true passions. The safety and security in unconditional love allows your heart to dream and discover your true purpose.

How in the world does this relate to cooking?

I've always enjoyed the kitchen, and I've always been a pretty good cook. But the safety of unconditional, covenant love has given me the opportunity to discover my passion. It has taught me to embrace my truth and my purpose and to commit myself to being the best I can be.

For me, that passion is cooking with love. It's sharing my heart with you in every dish, every recipe, every story. The love of my life has unlocked things in me that have enriched my life. I wish that for you. More than cooking a great meal, my desire is that you find your passion and allow your heart to blossom. May you find and embrace unconditional love. I have, and it has made all the difference in the world.

EASY EVERYDAY BEEF WELLINGTON

Remember what I said about filet mignon? Take that up several notches, and you have beef wellington. This is quite an intimidating dish, but it's much easier than you think. In fact, we have it for dinner on weeknights sometimes. Instead of making a filling with a pâté consistency, I like it a little heartier. So I make it with chopped vegetables instead. You can try it both ways and see what you think.

Directions

1. Preheat oven to 425 degrees F.
2. Coat the bottom of a skillet with olive oil and heat over medium-high heat until hot. Add garlic, onion, and mushrooms and cook until they begin to soften.
3. Add salt, pepper, rosemary, thyme, and parsley. Cook until onion is translucent and mushrooms begin to brown. Add olive oil as needed while cooking if the mixture begins to dry out. When mixture is done, put in separate bowl and set aside.
4. Over medium heat, add an additional 2–3 tablespoons of olive oil to the same skillet.
5. Season top side of steaks with salt and pepper. Place steaks seasoned-side down in the skillet and allow to sear for 2–3 minutes. Season the other side of the steaks before turning over. Remove from heat once seared (2–3 minutes per side)

Serves 2

INGREDIENTS

olive oil, for sautéing

2 tablespoons garlic, minced

1 yellow onion, chopped

1 cup chopped baby portobello mushrooms

salt and pepper to taste

1 tablespoon rosemary

1 tablespoon thyme

1 tablespoon parsley

2 individual filet mignon steaks

1 puff pastry, thawed

2 slices prosciutto

2 tablespoons Dijon mustard

1 egg wash (1 egg plus 2 tablespoons water)

6. Roll out puff pastry with a lightly floured rolling pin to create a larger rectangle. Cut pastry in half.

7. For each half, assemble as follows: Place 1 slice of prosciutto on pastry. Then add 1 tablespoon of the mushroom/onion filling. Brush Dijon mustard on both sides of steak and place on top of the prosciutto and filling.

8. Use egg wash to moisten the edges of the puff pastry. Fold the puff pastry over and around the steak until it is completely enclosed. Use additional egg wash to ensure the puff pastry stays closed at the seams.

9. Place pastry-wrapped steaks on a baking sheet, seam-side down, and cover top and sides of puff pastry with egg wash. With a fork, poke small steam vents in the top of the pastry.

10. Bake in oven for 20–25 minutes for desired doneness. (Do not cook steak past medium, or the filets will get very mad at you!)

11. Let steak rest for 10 minutes before cutting.

HERB-CRUSTED PRIME RIB

Serves 6–8

I've already stated that I could never be a vegetarian. This dish is one of the main reasons why. When merging the preparation of classic and contemporary dishes, special occasions are a big deal. That's where a standing rib roast comes in. This is a must in every cook's arsenal. You can switch up the herbs that you use and make it your own. After all, that's what Calibama cooking is all about—making it your own!

INGREDIENTS

For the herb crust:

- ¼ cup olive oil
- 2 tablespoons minced garlic
- 2 tablespoons parsley flakes
- 2 tablespoons basil
- 2 tablespoons thyme leaves
- 2 tablespoons rosemary leaves
- 1 tablespoon kosher salt
- ½ tablespoon fresh ground pepper

For the roast:

- 1 (4-pound) standing rib roast, bone in or bone out
- 10–12 garlic cloves, cut up (not minced)
- several fresh herbs: basil, thyme, tarragon, rosemary
- olive oil, for drizzling

Directions

1. Preheat oven to 325 degrees.
2. Combine all ingredients for the herb crust and set aside.
3. Insert a paring knife or a steak knife approximately 1 inch into the meat all over the top. Insert pieces of garlic cloves into the one-inch openings created with the knife.
4. Place fresh herbs and additional garlic cloves at bottom of baking dish and drizzle with olive oil.
5. Completely cover roast with herb crust, top and sides.
6. Insert meat thermometer in center of roast. If using bone-in roast, be sure thermometer does not touch bone.
7. Bake on lower oven rack until thermometer reads 10 degrees below your desired internal temperature. Remove from oven and allow roast to stand for 15–20 minutes. Roast will continue cooking and temperature will rise approximately 10 degrees.

TIPS

★ It is very easy to overcook a roast. Taking it out of the oven 10 degrees before it reaches your desired doneness is key to getting a perfectly cooked.

★ Letting the roast stand after removing it from the oven is crucial to a juicy roast. When you let the roast stand, the juices come together and stay in the roast.

★ I recommend cooking the roast to medium doneness. Anything past that, you're really missing out on the best flavor possible. Trust me . . . even if you're not used to eating a steak medium, just try it.

COUNTRY FRIED STEAK AND GRAVY

Serves 6

My grandma used to make this all the time. In the summers when I was with my grandparents, it felt like she made it every day (at least three days a week). So it should come as no surprise that I've included it in this cookbook. I do make my gravy a little different. Grandma didn't use portobello mushrooms or chopped onions. Country folks just use broth and flour! I don't think Grandma would be upset.

INGREDIENTS

neutral oil, for frying and for gravy

2–3 pounds round steak, tenderized and cut into cubes (also known as cube steak)

steak seasoning of your choice

2 cups flour

1 cup buttermilk

For the gravy:

1 yellow onion, chopped

1 cup baby portobello mushrooms, sliced

½ cup flour (depending on thickness desired for gravy)

4 cups beef broth

Directions

1. In a large skillet, heat ½ to 1 inch of oil over medium-high heat.
2. Season meat with steak seasoning.
3. In a large bowl, combine flour and another 4 tablespoons steak seasoning. Pour buttermilk into another large bowl.
4. Dredge seasoned steak in buttermilk, shake to remove the excess, then coat with seasoned flour.
5. Place steak in skillet and fry 3–4 minutes per side. The meat will not take long to cook.
6. Remove steak and drain on a paper towel. Drain oil from skillet, leaving 4 tablespoon of oil in pan for the gravy.
7. Add onion and mushrooms to skillet and cook until soft.

8. Sprinkle flour on softened vegetables, starting with 3–4 tablespoons. Increase amount of flour depending on how thick you want the gravy. Use extra olive oil if necessary to moisten vegetables after flour has been added.

9. When flour has absorbed into the vegetables, add beef broth, 1 cup at a time, and stir to combine. Bring to a boil and allow gravy to thicken. To thicken gravy even more, dissolve 1–2 tablespoons of flour in broth and stir into the gravy pan.

10. Serve steak topped with gravy.

Me: "Mama you make the best candied yams in the world. What's your secret?"

Mom: "You like my candied yams? I guess I better pay attention next time and figure out what I did!"

∽

Me: "How do you know when the food is done, Grandma?"

Grandma: "Taste it, baby!"

MOTHER'S DAY

When you grow up in a family with a lot of women and go to church all the time, Mother's Day is its own event.

At my church, we had Communion on the second Sunday of every month. (I don't know why it wasn't on the first Sunday, but that's not the point of this story. Stick with me). If you're familiar with Black church culture, you know that Communion means white dresses (at least that's what it meant back in the seventies and eighties. I don't know what's going on now.)

So on the second Sunday of every month for as long as I can remember I wore a white dress. When I got grown and started going to a less-rule-oriented church, I think I made some sort of secret deal with myself to never wear a white dress again.

Mom and me - 1987

Mother's Day is the second Sunday of May, and my grandma always said, "You're supposed to wear white on Mother's Day." Now I have done some checking, and I don't know where she got this from. She may have just made it up. But regardless, it was her world, she was the first lady, she was the matriarch, and she said you wear white on Mother's Day, period. Since it was the second Sunday anyway, I didn't really argue. It didn't matter.

So fast-forward to my less-rule-oriented church now as an adult. I don't own a white dress. I haven't for years (you know why). But on Mother's Day, to honor my grandma, I always try to wear white. Now, to stay true to myself, I still won't wear a white dress, but I've got various great white pants and things that I wear on Mother's Day that make me remember her. That's my Calibama style: white for Grandma, pants for me.

My Grandma - 1991

LAMB CHOPS IN MADEIRA WINE SAUCE

Serves 4

INGREDIENTS

olive oil, for sautéing

4 lamb chops, fat trimmed

salt and pepper to taste

1 cup all-purpose flour, plus 2 tablespoons for sauce

1 cup Madeira wine or cooking sherry

1½ cups beef broth, divided

2 tablespoons flour

*M*adeira wine is the key to this recipe. Its sweet and savory flavor profile takes lamb chops to another level. If you're leery of lamb, don't be. It's a lot like beef. Don't overcook it, or it will be tough and chewy. You can make the wine sauce thin, or you can make it Calibama style—thick like gravy.

Directions

1. On the bottom of a sauté pan, heat a thin layer of olive oil over medium heat.
2. Season lamb chops on both sides with salt and pepper. Dredge the seasoned lamb chops in 1 cup flour and place in the skillet to brown.
3. Cook lamb chops 3–4 minutes per side and remove. Do not cook completely, just to about 60 percent done.
4. Add the wine to the bottom of the pan, stirring up the bits for flavor. Slowly add 1 cup of the beef broth. Bring to a boil.
5. In a small bowl, combine 2 tablespoons flour with the remaining ½ cup beef broth. Whisk together well.
6. Slowly add the beef broth and flour mixture to the sauté pan, whisking constantly as the sauce thickens.
7. Return lamb chops to pan. Continue cooking over medium-low heat for an additional 5–7 minutes until lamb reaches desired doneness. I suggest medium, with a warm pink center.

SAUSAGE-STUFFED PORTOBELLO MUSHROOM CAPS

*T*his is one of the exceptions to my meat-loving tendencies, maybe because even though the base is a portobello mushroom, it's stuffed with sausage. I guess that makes it still a meat-lover's dish! Here's the cool part about this dish: you can make it with baby bellas for a great appetizer.

Directions

Prepare the mushrooms:

1. Preheat oven to 325 degrees F.
2. Clean out the inside of the portobello mushroom caps.
3. In a small bowl, combine ¼ cup olive oil and wine. Brush the mixture onto the mushroom caps.

Make the stuffing:

1. In a skillet, heat more olive oil over medium-high heat until hot. Add baby portobellos, onion, and garlic. Cook until soft.
2. Add seasoned pepper, chili powder, and salt to skillet. Add all the sausage. Mix well and cook together until almost done.
3. Stir in ⅔ cup panko bread crumbs; combine thoroughly.
4. Remove skillet from heat and stir in cheeses and

Serves 6

INGREDIENTS

6 large portobello mushroom caps, cleaned

¼ cup olive oil, plus more for sautéing

2 tablespoons Madeira cooking wine

For the stuffing:

2 cups baby portobello mushrooms, chopped

1 yellow onion, chopped

2 cloves garlic, minced or chopped

1 teaspoon seasoned pepper

1 teaspoon chili powder

½ teaspoon salt

½ pound hot ground sausage

½ pound sweet ground sausage

1 cup panko bread crumbs, divided

1 cup havarti cheese

1 cup parmesan cheese

2 tablespoons parsley, fresh or dried

parsley; combine well, allowing cheese to melt. (Sneak a taste to be sure you like it; adjust with additional cheeses and so on until you get it just the way you like it.)

Assemble stuffed mushrooms:

1. Stuff portobello mushroom caps with filling. Sprinkle remaining ⅓ cup panko bread crumbs on top. Drizzle with any remaining wine mixture.
2. Bake in oven for 50 minutes.

PORK ENCHILADAS VERDE

Serves 6

I can't lie: this recipe is labor-intensive, but it is so worth the time and effort to roast your own tomatillos to make your own verde sauce. It is absolutely amazing and flavor-packed. And another bonus: any leftover pork can be used to make tacos the next day.

Directions

Make the verde sauce:

1. Preheat oven to 450 degrees F.
2. Place tomatillos, poblanos, and jalapeños on a large baking sheet. Broil for 3 minutes on top rack of oven, until outside of peppers begins to char.
3. Move baking sheet to middle rack and bake until soft, 8–10 minutes. Remove and allow to cool slightly. (Peel skin off of peppers if you like.) Wait for the pork to finish cooking before continuing on to next step.
4. Place tomatillos, peppers, onion, garlic, salt, and juice from cooked tenderloin in blender. Blend until smooth. To thin sauce out, add an additional ½ cup water or broth.

Make the pork:

1. Preheat oven to 375 degrees F.
2. In a large, oven-safe, lidded skillet, heat olive oil over medium-high heat
3. In a small bowl, combine minced garlic, cilantro, salt, and pepper.

INGREDIENTS

For the verde sauce:

1½ pounds tomatillos, cut into quarters

2 poblano peppers, seeds removed, cut into quarters (if unavailable, use additional jalapeños)

2 jalapeño peppers, seeds removed, cut into quarters

½ cup juice from cooked pork tenderloin

1 cup diced white onion

3 cloves garlic

1 teaspoon salt

For the pork tenderloin seasoning:

¼ cup olive oil

3 garlic cloves, minced

3 tablespoons cilantro

1 teaspoon kosher salt

2 teaspoons black pepper

2 pounds pork tenderloin

1 cup water or chicken broth

For assembly:

10–12 corn tortillas

queso fresco cheese

cojita cheese

4. Slice 1 inch down the middle of the pork tenderloin and place the seasoning mixture inside. Reserve 2 tablespoons of the mixture to rub onto the outside of the pork.
5. Add pork to skillet and sear for approximately 4 minutes on each side until golden brown.
6. Remove skillet from heat and pour in water or broth. Cover with a lid and roast in oven for 20–25 minutes.
7. When pork is finished, let stand in skillet with lid on for approximately 10 minutes to keep the juices in.
8. Reserve approximately ½ cup of the juices from the pork dish to use in the verde sauce.
9. Chop up pork and prepare to fill enchiladas.

For assembly:

1. Turn oven heat up to 400 degrees F.
2. Warm tortillas in microwave or pass through hot corn oil.
3. Dip warmed tortillas in verde sauce.
4. Fill each tortilla with 1–2 tablespoons chopped pork (or as much as you want!) and crumbled queso fresco.
5. Cover enchiladas with extra verde sauce and additional cheese (if desired).
6. Bake for 15–20 minutes.
7. Remove from oven and crumble fresh cojita cheese on top.

SMOTHERED PORK CHOPS

Serves 4–6

This is what my grandma made on the days she didn't make country fried steak and gravy. I think I could eat smothered pork chops at least once or twice a week. Add some mashed potatoes or white rice, and honey, chile! That's good eatin'!

Directions

1. In a large skillet, heat ½ inch of neutral frying oil over medium-high heat until hot.
2. In a small bowl, combine onion powder, garlic powder, salt, and pepper.
3. Season pork chops with 2–3 tablespoons of the seasoning mixture.
4. In a medium bowl, combine 1 cup of flour with 2 additional tablespoons of the same seasoning mix.
5. Dredge the seasoned pork chops in the seasoned flour and add to skillet. Fry until golden brown. Do not cook them all the way—just until they're pretty!
6. Remove pork chops from oil and set aside.
7. In the same skillet, combine celery, green pepper, onion, and garlic. Reduce heat to medium and cook until vegetables become soft.
8. Add remaining 2 tablespoons flour to vegetables and stir to coat. Add an additional 1–2 tablespoons of the seasoning mixture. Continue stirring until flour has been completely absorbed by the oil.
9. Add chicken broth and bring to a slight boil, stirring continuously.

INGREDIENTS

- neutral oil, frying oil
- 3 tablespoons onion powder
- 3 tablespoons garlic powder
- 2 tablespoons salt
- 1 tablespoon black pepper
- 6–8 bone-in center-cut pork chops
- 1 cup all-purpose flour, plus 2 tablespoons for gravy
- 3 celery stalks, chopped
- 1 green bell pepper, chopped
- 1 yellow onion, chopped
- 2 tablespoons garlic, minced
- 3–4 cups chicken broth

TIPS

★ Instead of simmering the pork chops in the skillet in step 10, you can bake them with the gravy in a covered dish at 400 degrees for 20 minutes (until fully done).

★ If you'd like your pork chops to have a little spice to them, you can add some red pepper flakes to the pork chops and/or the gravy.

★ You can make your gravy as thick or as thin as you'd like. Adjust the amount of flour you add to the vegetables to thicken up your gravy.

★ Using chicken broth instead of water makes your gravy even more flavorful.

10. Return pork chops to skillet. Simmer over medium-low heat until chops are done completely, about 20 minutes.

EXTRA MEATY HEARTY LASAGNA

*T*his is a pretty easy meal to make. It's just a big assembly project. I frequently make a big batch of my meaty marinara sauce and freeze it so that whenever the mood strikes, I can jump in and assemble this lasagna. Be warned: my marinara sauce really makes this dish filling. If you've got a big family or a lot of hungry folks coming, this is the ticket!

Serves 8–10

INGREDIENTS

1 cup cottage cheese

1 cup ricotta cheese

½ recipe Lori's Meaty Marinara Sauce

12–15 uncooked lasagna noodles

1 cup italian-style shredded cheese

Directions

1. Preheat oven to 375 degrees F.
2. In a bowl, combine the cottage and ricotta cheeses.
3. Assemble the lasagna in a 9-by-13-inch baking dish follow this layering guide:
   - layer 1: sauce, uncooked lasagna noodles, cheese mixture, shredded cheese
   - layer 2: sauce, uncooked lasagna noodles, cheese mixture, shredded cheese
   - layer 3: sauce, uncooked lasagna noodles, cheese mixture
4. Sprinkle remaining shredded cheese on top, cover with aluminum and bake for 30-45 minutes, until a toothpick or skewer can go through the entire dish.
5. Remove the foil and bake for an additional 10-15 minutes.
6. Remove from oven and let stand for 10-15 minutes before cutting.

LEMON BASIL CHICKEN

Serves 6–8

This recipe requires a lot of cutting and chopping. To save time, you can purchase precut vegetables from the produce department of your local grocery store. Yes, they will cost a touch more, but sometimes convenience is worth the price.

Directions

1. Preheat oven to 425 degrees F.
2. Season chicken with salt, pepper, and garlic powder. Drizzle with olive oil and incorporate seasonings into the chicken.
3. *Make the marinade/sauce:* In a medium bowl, combine ingredients for marinade/sauce with juice from lemon quarters. Combine well.
4. Coat the chicken with half of the marinade. Coat the sweet peppers, potatoes, and onions with the other half.
5. Spray a 9-by-13-inch baking dish lightly with cooking spray. Add the vegetables and spread out. Top with the chicken. Push the chicken pieces together closely so all of them fit into the baking dish. Place lemon quarters around the dish so the flavor bakes in.
6. Bake for 40–50 minutes until chicken is done.

INGREDIENTS

- 10–12 pieces of chicken (I recommend boneless, skinless thighs)
- salt and pepper
- 2 tablespoons garlic powder
- olive oil, for drizzling
- 4–6 lemons, quartered and lightly juiced (¼ to ⅓ cup), divided
- 10 small sweet peppers, sliced, seeds removed
- 7–10 medium potatoes, diced into bite-size pieces
- 2 large yellow onions, sliced

For the marinade/sauce:

- 1 stick butter, softened
- 1 cup olive oil
- ¼ cup minced garlic
- ⅓ cup basil, chopped
- salt, pepper, and garlic powder to taste

CAJUN CHICKEN PASTA

Serves 4–6

This is my go-to meal. I can get this from stove to table in twenty to twenty-five minutes. Depending on how quickly you need to get it on the table, you can use rotisserie chicken with the meat pulled off the bone or cook your own chicken. And you can make the sauce as spicy or as mild as you'd like. My family absolutely loves this meal. It's always a winner.

INGREDIENTS

- olive oil, for sautéing
- 1 red bell pepper, sliced
- 1 green bell pepper, sliced
- 1 yellow onion, sliced
- 1½ pounds boneless, skinless chicken breasts, cubed
- 5 tablespoons Cajun seasoning, divided
- 1½ cups heavy whipping cream
- ½ cup all-purpose flour
- ½ cup chicken broth
- salt to taste (optional)
- 3 cups cooked pasta (reserve 1 cup pasta water)

Directions

1. In a large skillet, heat olive oil over medium heat.
2. Add the bell peppers and onion. Season with 2 tablespoons Cajun seasoning while they cook.
3. In a large bowl, coat the chicken with the remaining Cajun seasoning.
4. When the vegetables are soft, add the seasoned chicken to the skillet. Use additional olive oil if needed to keep the chicken and vegetables moist.
5. When chicken is 80 to 90 percent done, slowly add cream to the chicken and vegetables.
6. In a medium bowl, dissolve the flour in the chicken broth. Slowly stir mixture into pan. Continue cooking and bring to a boil until sauce is thickened. If necessary, add some of the reserved pasta water to reach your desired consistency for the sauce.
7. Serve over cooked pasta.

SEAFOOD

Grilled, poached, baked, broiled, fried, blackened, sautéed—there are endless ways to prepare seafood. The delicate nature of fish lends itself to so many options. Experimenting with fish can be such fun and extremely rewarding.

I've had some pretty cool accidents happen in the kitchen with fish recipes. Over the years, I've grown super-fond of swordfish. It took me several years to try it, and now I can't get enough of it. My favorite swordfish recipe is included, and I hope you try it.

My parents and me - 1987

FISH FRIES

Have I told y'all how much my daddy liked to go fishing? My whole childhood, we always had a boat. We would go fishing in the Sacramento River. I actually enjoyed it . . . as long as I didn't have to touch any fish or bait! In true Daddy-style, my daddy would bait every hook for me and take my fish off the line.

Frequently, my dad and his friends would go deep-sea fishing in the Pacific Ocean. This was an all-day affair. He would leave before sunrise and get back late in the evening. When he would catch ling cod, I was in heaven! By now, you know that my people are from the country. So we fried it. And Lawd ha' mercy! (Translation: Lord have mercy!) That was the best stuff.

In the late summer, my daddy would go back to Mobile on a fishing trip with my uncle. Daddy used to catch gulf shrimp. Now if you have never had gulf shrimp, something is missing in your life experience. That gulf shrimp from the Mobile Bay was sweet, succulent, and tender. Daddy would freeze it after he caught it; wrap it in foil and box it up; and bring it back home with him. (I told y'all we were country!)

The shrimp made the trip every time. Not one soul was lost. And there was no smell of fish in his luggage. (These are just the things that happen when your parents are from the South.) Once Daddy and the shrimp made it home, he and my mama would cook up the best fried shrimp I've ever had.

My parents were very hospitable about fish and BBQ, but we didn't share the gulf shrimp! That was just for the three of us. I think this is where my love of fried shrimp came from.

I've expanded my culinary skills to include pan-searing and blackening, but my favorite way to eat fish will always be fried, baby, fried!

Frying cod in cast iron just like my Daddy taught me.

PAN-SEARED SWORDFISH WITH GREEK SAUCE

Makes 4 swordfish steaks

*T*he first time I made this dish, my husband's look of sheer delight made my day. There's a Greek restaurant that used to make a version of this that he absolutely loved. Well, suffice it to say, when I finished with this dish and added my special Calibama touches, he could barely remember the name of that restaurant!

INGREDIENTS

olive oil (to coat the bottom of the pan)

4 swordfish steaks

salt and pepper

For the Greek sauce:

½ cup lemon juice

¼ cup olive oil

2 tablespoons oregano

1 tablespoon minced garlic

1 teaspoon salt

½ teaspoon black pepper

Directions

1. Preheat the oven to 400 degrees F.
2. Coat an oven-safe skillet with olive oil and heat over medium-high heat.
3. Season one side of the fish with salt and pepper and place, seasoned-side down, in the skillet to sear. Sear the meat on one side for 3–5 minutes until golden brown. Turn the meat over, remove skillet from heat, and add 1–2 tablespoons of olive oil to the pan.
4. Place pan in 400 degree preheated oven for 8–9 minutes. Fish will not take a long time to cook, and you don't want to overcook it.
5. While the fish is in the oven, prepare the Greek sauce by combining all ingredients in a saucepan over medium heat. Do not bring the sauce to a complete boil; just warm it thoroughly.
6. When the fish is done, remove from oven and top with warmed Greek sauce.

CREAMY CAJUN LOBSTER AND SHRIMP FETTUCCINE

SERVES **4**

You can use as much or as little as Cajun seasoning as you like. As you can see, I use quite a bit . . . but it makes me happy. You should adjust the amount to suit your taste. You can also get really creative with what shellfish you add to this. Add some crab too! It can only get better.

INGREDIENTS

olive oil

1 pound shrimp, peeled and deveined

4–6 small lobster tails

⅓ cup Cajun seasoning, divided

1 yellow onion, chopped

1 cup sliced baby portobello mushrooms

2 garlic cloves, minced or chopped

3 tablespoons flour

3 cups half-and-half

1 cup chicken broth

1 pound fettuccine, cooked according to package instructions

Directions

1. Preheat oven to 450 degrees F. Heat a skillet with enough olive oil to cover the bottom over medium heat.

2. In a large bowl, lightly coat shrimp and lobster with olive oil. Sprinkle with 2–3 tablespoons Cajun seasoning.

3. Place lobster on a baking sheet lightly sprayed with cooking oil. Broil in center of oven for 6–8 minutes. They will be opaque white when done. Do not overcook.

4. Add onion and mushrooms to warmed skillet with olive oil. When vegetables begin to soften, add the garlic and season with Cajun seasoning.

5. Add shrimp to skillet and cook until they begin to turn white. The shrimp should be translucent and almost completely opaque before moving on to the next step.

6. Sprinkle 2 tablespoons flour on mixture in skillet. Stir until dissolved. Slow pour in half-and-half and ½ cup chicken broth.

SEA FOOD

7. Dissolve the remaining tablespoon of flour into remaining ½ cup chicken broth and add slowly to pan to thicken sauce as desired. If more Cajun seasoning is desired, add more now.

8. When lobster tails are done, serve on top of fettuccine and shrimp.

BLACKENED SALMON WITH LEMON HERB BUTTER

SERVES 4

INGREDIENTS

5 tablespoons clarified butter
2 pounds salmon fillets
5–6 tablespoons seafood seasoning
1 stick unsalted butter, softened
1 teaspoon kosher salt
1 teaspoon herb seasoning
juice of half a lemon

This is a really healthy way to get excellent flavor into your fish and have a nice crisp exterior without frying. I make this for friends and family with health concerns. Served with a side of sautéed spinach and green swiss chard, it's a real winner!

Directions

1. Heat a large skillet over medium heat. Add clarified butter and melt.
2. Generously season salmon fillets on both sides with seafood seasoning.
3. Place seasoned fillets in hot clarified butter in skillet. Cook on each side for 3–4 minutes until outside is slightly charred (blackened) and desired doneness is reached. If the outside chars before the fish is cooked to your desired doneness, turn the heat down and continue cooking.
4. In a medium bowl, combine the softened butter, salt, herb seasoning, and lemon juice. Combine well.
5. Remove fillets from skillet. Place a small dollop of lemon herb butter on top of each.

I LOVE ME SOME GRITS

Everybody has their go-to food. For me, it's grits. When I'm sick or just not feeling well, I fix a bowl of grits, and suddenly everything is better.

Oddly enough, my Virginia-born-and-raised husband is not a fan of grits. How does that work? The Virginia boy doesn't like grits, but the California girl loves them?! It's a Calibama miracle!

When I was growing up, I thought everybody ate grits. I mean, duh! Imagine my surprise when I found out that quite a few folks have never had them, and some who have had them just don't like grits. They must not have been cooked right!

When it comes to grits, I'm something of a purist. Perfect grits:

- don't need cheese
- don't need sugar
- don't need gravy

If they're cooked right, grits need two things and two things only: salt and butter.

There is but one exception to my purist philosophy: shrimp and grits. Shrimp and grits requires cheese grits. But that's the only time cheese is absolutely necessary. While I am quite fond of cheese grits, outside of this one dish, there is no need to mess with the perfection of creamy grits.

That's just my two cents!

SPICY SHRIMP AND GRITS

*T*his is by far my personal favorite meal. I love everything about it: the shrimp, the bacon, the grits, and the spice. Shrimp and grits is kind of like chili: everybody has their own special way of preparing it—some make it creamy, some use sausage, some add lots of various fresh peppers. This is why I enjoy ordering shrimp and grits when we travel. I look forward to tasting everybody's special touch.

Directions

1. In a large skillet over medium-high heat, cook bacon until crispy. When bacon is done, remove and set aside. Leave 3 tablespoons rendered fat in pan.

2. While bacon is cooking, in a large bowl, coat shrimp with olive oil. Add chili powder, paprika, cayenne, and thyme and combine to fully coat shrimp with seasonings.

3. Cook onion and garlic in 2 tablespoons bacon fat until soft. Add seasoned shrimp. Cook until shrimp is about 90 percent done, 4–6 minutes.

4. Pour in cooking sherry and continue cooking on medium heat. Add bacon and continue cooking.

5. Remove skillet from heat when shrimp are completely done (they will be white when finished).

6. Stir shredded gouda cheese into prepared grits. Serve shrimp over grits.

Serves 6

INGREDIENTS

1 pound bacon, diced

2 pounds shrimp, peeled and deveined

olive oil

2 tablespoons chili powder

2 tablespoons paprika

1 tablespoon cayenne

1 tablespoon thyme

1 yellow onion, chopped

2 cloves garlic, chopped

1 cup cooking sherry (or any red wine you enjoy)

1 cup shredded gouda cheese

2–3 cups grits, prepared according to package instructions

CRAB-STUFFED FLOUNDER

Serves 4

*F*lounder is a very gentle fish. This recipe is flavorful but not overpowering. The garlic cream sauce brings it all together in a beautiful way that will make you smile.

Directions

Make the crab filling:

1. In a medium bowl, combine all filling ingredients except for the egg and stir well to combine.
2. Stir in the egg, ensuring that it is fully incorporated into the mixture.

Stuff the flounder:

1. Preheat oven to 350 degrees F. Spray a 9-by-13-inch baking dish with cooking oil.
2. Season the flounder on both sides with salt and pepper.
3. Stuff approximately ¼ cup of the crab filling into the center of the flounder filet.
4. Roll flounder with the crab mixture in it. Place in prepared baking dish. Bake in oven for 20–30 minutes. (You'll make the garlic cream sauce while it cooks.)
5. Turn on broiler and broil for 4–5 minutes on high. Set aside until ready to serve.

INGREDIENTS

For the crab filling:

- 2 cups cooked crabmeat
- ½ yellow onion, chopped
- 2 medium sweet peppers, chopped
- ⅓ cup bread crumbs
- 2 tablespoons minced garlic
- 1 tablespoon seasoned pepper
- 1 tablespoon chili powder
- 1 teaspoon paprika
- 1 tablespoon olive oil
- salt to taste
- 1 egg

For the flounder:

- 4 flounder fillets, thinly sliced
- salt and pepper to taste
- paprika, for garnish

For the garlic cream sauce:

- 2 tablespoons minced garlic
- 2 cups heavy whipping cream
- ⅓ cup all-purpose flour
- ½ cup chicken broth
- 2 tablespoons garlic salt

Make the garlic cream sauce:

1. While fish is cooking, in a medium-size skillet, heat 1–2 tablespoons olive oil over medium heat.
2. Add the garlic and cook until it becomes soft and fragrant.
3. Add the whipping cream.
4. Dissolve 3–5 tablespoons flour in chicken broth. Use more or less flour depending on how thick you want the sauce to be.
5. Add the chicken broth mixture to the skillet, whisking constantly, and bring to a boil. The sauce will start to thicken.
6. Cover broiled flounder with garlic cream sauce and garnish with sprinkled paprika.

LOBSTER AND SHRIMP ROLLS

MAKES 8 ROLLS

In New England, lobster rolls are a tradition. In true Calibama style, I can't leave well enough alone. Since shrimp is one of my favorite foods, and shrimp and lobster are cousins (in my world at least), I decided to combine the two. Lots of recipes only use mayonnaise, but that's boring! I like to add some Dijon, green onions, and a lot of seasoning. Hook it up like you like it.

INGREDIENTS

- 6 (4-ounce) lobster tails, cleaned and ready to use
- 1 pound shrimp, peeled, deveined, tails removed
- 6 tablespoons butter, divided
- 4 tablespoons seafood seasoning, divided
- 1 cup mayonnaise
- 1 tablespoon Dijon mustard
- 3 green onions, finely chopped
- 3 celery stalks, chopped
- 2–4 tablespoons seafood seasoning (such as Old Bay)
- 8 split-top rolls

Directions

1. Heat oven broiler to 450 degrees F.
2. Season lobster tails and shrimp with 2 tablespoons butter and approximately 2 tablespoons of your favorite seafood seasoning.
3. Broil on middle rack for 10–12 minutes. Seafood will be opaque white when it is done.
4. Remove seafood from oven and allow to cool. Chop into bite-size pieces.
5. In a large bowl, stir together lobster, shrimp, mayo, mustard, green onions, and celery. Season with remaining 2 tablespoons of seafood seasoning (more or less to taste).
6. In a skillet, toast rolls over medium heat with remaining 4 tablespoons butter.
7. Fill with lobster and shrimp filling.

CILANTRO LIME SHRIMP TACOS

Serves 4–6

W ho doesn't love Taco Tuesday? This girl loves tacos any day of the week! Tacos go up to a whole new level with cilantro and lime. This is another one of those quick recipes that won't take forever to make, but you will seriously enjoy it.

INGREDIENTS

For the shrimp tacos:

2 tablespoons olive oil, plus more for drizzling

2 shallots, sliced

1 clove garlic, minced

1½ pounds shrimp, peeled, deveined, tails removed

1 tablespoon cumin

1 tablespoon chili powder

1 teaspoon cayenne pepper (optional)

3 tablespoons chopped cilantro

4–6 taco shells, soft or crispy

For the cilantro lime sour cream:

1½ cups sour cream

2 tablespoons cilantro

juice of ½ lime

Directions

1. In a large skillet, heat olive oil over medium-high heat.
2. Add shallots and garlic and cook until soft and fragrant.
3. In a large bowl, coat the shrimp with a drizzle of olive oil and stir in cumin, chili powder, and cayenne (if using).
4. Add shrimp to skillet and cook until shrimp are opaque white.
5. Stir in the cilantro.
6. In a small bowl, combine all ingredients for the cilantro lime sour cream and set aside.
7. Assemble tacos in taco shells and top with cilantro lime sour cream.

TIP

★ I like to use McCormick's Grill Mates Mojito Lime seasoning for this recipe. For that reason, this is one of my quickest dinner recipes. All you need is a pack or two of the seasoning and you can get dinner on the table in under thirty minutes. But you don't have to use just Mojito Lime seasoning. You can use any flavor profile you like to make this dish your own.

SIDES AND VEGGIES

There are times when the side dishes almost taste better than anything else on your plate! You know, like after Thanksgiving, when you just want some greens, dressing, and corn. I'm always a sucker for the potato side dishes. Be it mashed potatoes, sweet potatoes, or even french fries, I keep coming back for more.

LORIOUS MACARONI AND CHEESE

SERVES 4–8

Mac and cheese is everybody's favorite. The obvious question becomes, what makes this recipe so special? Well, the answer is quite simple: this is pretty much how my grandma made it. She made the best mac and cheese in the world. The egg is optional, but Grandma always put it in hers. Sometimes I leave it out when my kids are too hungry to wait for it finish baking. Whether you include or exclude the egg, you'll love this classic mac and cheese. Thanks, Grandma!

INGREDIENTS

½ cup (1 stick) butter

½ cup all-purpose flour

2 cups half-and-half (or heavy whipping cream, if you're feeling it)

1 tablespoon garlic powder

1 teaspoon salt

1 teaspoon pepper

4 cups shredded cheese

⅓ cup sour cream

1 pound elbow macaroni, cooked (reserve 1 cup pasta water)

2 eggs, lightly beaten (optional)

Directions

1. Preheat oven to 375 degrees F.
2. In a stockpot, melt butter over medium heat. Whisk in flour until smooth.
3. Slowly pour in half-and-half; continue cooking and stirring until mixture begins to thicken.
4. Add garlic powder, salt and pepper. Continue stirring.
5. Add shredded cheese and stir well until combined.
6. Stir in sour cream
7. Fold in cooked macaroni. Add reserved pasta water ⅓ cup at a time until desired consistency is achieved.
8. If using eggs, stir into macaroni and cheese mixture.
9. Transfer to a 9-by-13-inch pan and bake until the top is bubbly, 25–30 minutes.

TIP

★ When you finish boiling your noodles, be sure to set aside some of the pasta water. It will help your mac and cheese be even creamier. Right before you put it in the oven or serve it up from the stove, stir in that pasta water in and taste the magic.

REFINED LITTLE PALATES

Let me start by saying I have the best children in the world, period. (Every mom thinks that!) I have been so blessed to be mom to three of the most amazing blessings around. I have a dear cousin who calls her children gems. I think she's onto something. My gems sparkle and shine, and they make my life richer than it ever could have been.

Having said all of that, when you enjoy cooking as much as I do, and you like to make everything from scratch, consider this your official warning: children develop refined little palates that only you can satisfy! There are so many things my children have thought they didn't like until I made it from scratch with a little kiss of Mama's love, and it's become their favorite.

Richard, the oldest, is a huge fan of my mac and cheese and sweet potato pie. He was the only one of the three who knew my grandmother (she passed away before the others were born), and he is named after her father. So needless to say, she played an important role in his early life before she passed. It's somewhat ironic that I too loved my grandma's mac and cheese and sweet potato pie. Whenever I cook those items in particular, I always imagine myself sitting with her. I think those dishes conjure up Rich's favorite memories of her too.

Madison is my only daughter. Suffice it to say, she is well aware of her status as Daddy's girl and Mama's baby. She has the most refined of all the palates. She only wants Mama's homemade pesto and Mama's BBQ ribs with Chef Lorious seasoning and sauce. She wants her eggs cooked only with Chef Lorious house seasoning. She only eats Mama's mac and cheese . . . you get the picture. And don't get it twisted. She can tell if her mama cooked it or not! I always say she's my biggest fan and best taste-tester. She'll stick with you until it's just right.

Now Aiden is Mama's little love bug. He is the family baby, and he's not afraid to let you know. Aiden is our silly guy and always the life of the family party. There is never a dull moment with this kid! He is our grazer. For whatever reason, he doesn't like to just sit down and eat. He wants to taste a little bit of this and a little bit of that. My most rewarding moments are when he looks at me with his big brown eyes and little face and says, "Mommy, that's delicious!" Those words to me are the equivalent of hearing a European soccer commentator shout *"Goal!"*

These three refined palates have pushed me beyond my limits in the kitchen. They are always honest (Lord help me!) and always supportive. I complain sometimes about the hardships of children who know the different stages of caramelized onions and who can tell the difference between store-bought aioli and homemade. But the truth is that I wouldn't have it any other way!

SAUTÉED CABBAGE WITH BACON AND GARLIC

*C*abbage is a blessing in disguise. Few kids like cabbage (I was one of those kids). But then you bring garlic and bacon to the party, and all of a sudden, cabbage is amazing!

Directions

1. In a large skillet or Dutch oven over medium-high heat, cook bacon until crisp. Remove bacon and set aside, reserving rendered fat.
2. Add garlic and shallots to skillet and cook in 1–2 tablespoons rendered fat until just soft.
3. Add cabbage by the handful, allowing each to cook down slightly before adding the next batch. As you add the cabbage, add olive oil 1 tablespoon at a time as needed to help the cabbage cook down. Season with desired seasonings. Combine very well.
4. Cover dish and allow heat/steam to cook the cabbage down. Stir frequently to ensure all ingredients are combined and nothing sticks to the bottom.
5. Toss the cooked bacon on top as you serve the cabbage.

Serves 4–6

INGREDIENTS

1 pound bacon, diced

3 cloves garlic, minced

3 shallots, sliced

½ head cabbage, cut up

olive oil

seasoned salt and seasoned pepper to taste

TIPS

- When you cook cabbage, remember that it will wilt in the skillet. So initially, it will look like a mound of cabbage, but give it time, and it will settle down. It won't settle as much as spinach or collard greens, but it won't be nearly as big as it starts.
- Any pork fat will do here. In this recipe, I use bacon, but sausage works too. Especially italian-style or andouille sausage—*yum-my!*

LUCKY BLACK-EYED PEAS

SERVES 6–8

B*lack eyed-peas are a Southern staple. It's hard to find a Southern kitchen without black-eyed peas for New Year's. Folk history says they bring good luck in the year ahead. When you store black-eyed peas, they have a tendency to soak up the excess liquid in the bowl. So you may need to add a little chicken broth or water when you heat them up, but they'll still taste good.*

INGREDIENTS

1½ pounds bacon, in pieces
4 shallots, diced
3 cloves garlic, minced or chopped
1 tablespoon garlic powder
1 teaspoon cayenne pepper (optional)
6 cups chicken broth
6 cups black-eyed peas, fresh or frozen

Directions

1. In a large stockpot over medium-high heat, cook the bacon until almost done. It should not be crispy.
2. Add shallots and garlic to bacon and combine well.
3. Add garlic powder and cayenne pepper (if using) and continue cooking until shallots soften.
4. Add chicken broth and bring to a boil.
5. Stir in the black-eyed peas and bring back to a boil.
6. Once boiling, reduce heat to medium low, cover, and simmer for 1–2 hours, until peas are soft but not mushy.

GRANDMA'S COLLARD GREENS

Serves 6–8

INGREDIENTS

1 pound bacon, cut into pieces

2 garlic cloves, minced

1 tablespoon garlic powder

1 tablespoon onion powder

1 tablespoon salt

1 tablespoon black pepper

1 bunch collard greens, stems removed, leaves cut into shreds

4 cups chicken broth

2 tablespoons olive oil

If you read the introduction, you know I'm an Alabama girl who grew up in Northern California. You also know that Grandma and the church mothers are the best cooks that every existed. My grandma cooked her greens with ham hocks; I make mine with bacon. No particular reason—it just works better for me. But I swear, every time I make these greens, I feel like I'm sitting down talking with her.

Directions

1. In a large stockpot over medium-high heat, cook bacon pieces. Do not remove bacon or fat rendered from pot.
2. When bacon is done, add minced garlic, garlic powder, onion powder, salt, and pepper. Combine well.
3. Begin adding the cut-up collards to the pot, one handful at a time. Allow the greens to cook down in the bacon and seasoning mixture before adding more. Stir frequently.
4. When greens are bright and have started to wilt, begin adding chicken broth.
5. Bring to a boil, then reduce heat. Cover and simmer for several hours (at least 2).

TIP

★ Don't get lazy and skip the step where you remove the middle stems. Some folks won't eat greens with that stem in them. I've had them both ways, and without the stem is definitely best (in my opinion). And don't neglect the "pot liquor"—that is, the juice that is created in the pot as the greens cook. That is the best stuff ever. Add some corn bread to sop it up and OMG, it's like heaven on earth!

CRISPY GLAZED BRUSSELS SPROUTS

Serves 2–3

INGREDIENTS

peanut oil, for frying

2 cups brussels sprouts, cut into quarters, washed and fully dried

¼ cup honey

2 tablespoons lime juice

1 teaspoon red cayenne

1 cup cooked bacon, crumbled (reserve 2 tablespoons rendered fat)

*C*abbage and brussels sprouts are related, you know. Brussels sprouts are cabbage's little sister. And as with cabbage, I don't think you can find a kid who actually enjoys them (except for one of my daughter's friends). But something magical happens when you become an adult—if you have an open mind. You try them cooked a little different from how your mom made them, and you have a new favorite vegetable.

Directions

1. In a deep stockpot, heat 2 inches of peanut oil to 350 degrees.
2. Drop **dry** brussels sprouts in hot oil. Do not overcrowd pan. Fry until the ends of leaves start to turn brown and curl, 3–4 minutes.
3. Remove brussels sprouts from skillet and place on paper towels to drain excess oil.
4. In a large bowl, combine honey, lime juice, and red cayenne. Whisk together until well combined.
5. Add cooked brussels sprouts and crumbled bacon to bowl. (If desired, add 1–2 tablespoons of the reserved bacon fat for additional flavor.)
6. Toss sprouts and bacon in honey lime glaze until well coated. Serve immediately.

TIPS

★ Experiment with different flavors. Sometimes I put balsamic glaze on these sprouts. Sometimes it's honey with a cayenne kick. Sometimes it's candied pecans. You get the picture. Play around a little, and you may discover a new favorite.

★ The brussels sprouts need to be dry before you place them in hot oil. Any moisture in the sprouts will cause extreme popping. So trust me—be sure they are dry.

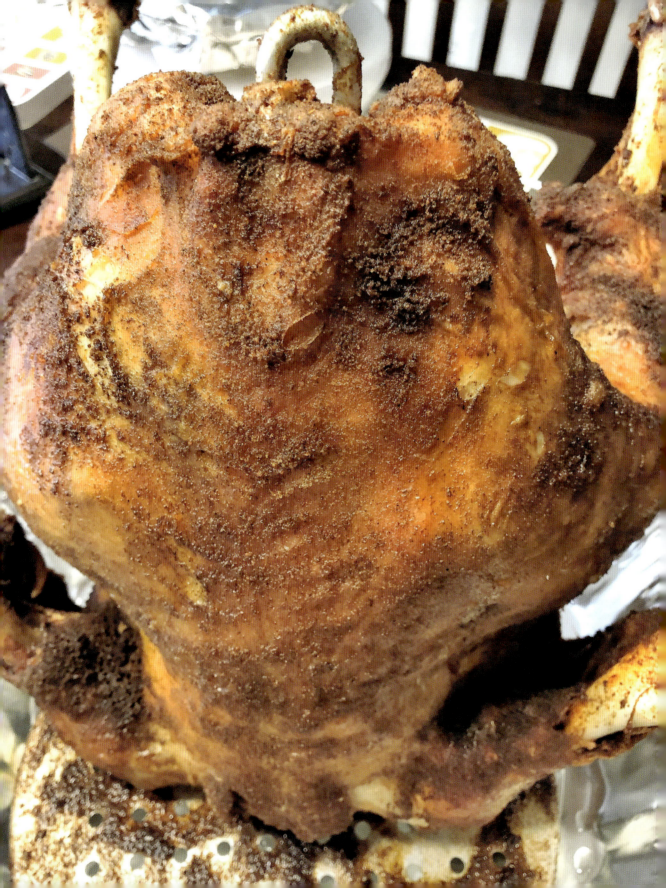

THANKSGIVING

It should come as no surprise that Thanksgiving is my favorite holiday. It is the Super Bowl for those of us who love to cook. I have been cooking Thanksgiving dinner for years, and I have no intention of stopping. My husband and I decided when we got married to have holidays at home so our children would remember it and so we could bring together both sides of our family. Everybody already knew each other, and it was a perfect way to be together at least once a year. The fact that I cook everything makes it easy for everyone to enjoy coming over.

I love cooking all of the food for Thanksgiving. I'll let someone bring something; it's not that serious! But I get such joy out of starting on Tuesday and cooking all the way through to Thursday (with a few naps in between). I've often asked myself why I do so much for this one day. I mean, three to four meats; ten or more sides; five to seven desserts . . . it's really overkill! After all these years, I've figured out why I love the cooking and why I love Thanksgiving so much. Here goes:

1. We open our home to family and friends for Thanksgiving, and I love to love people. My husband has a huge heart, and neither of us likes to see people we know alone on Thanksgiving. All holidays have their own level of importance, but something about the togetherness of Thanksgiving is just special. So we always take time to be sure we've thought about everyone in our circle, friends from church, extended family, and work friends, and we try to extend an invitation.

The thing about love is—it never runs out. It's the one thing in the world that has an endless supply. So we cook way too much food because we're never sure exactly how many people will show up. But whoever shows up, whether it's ten people or twenty-five (yes, we've had it happen), we never run out of anything.

2. Thanksgiving isn't overly commercialized. Every other holiday is about stuff—getting more stuff. But not Thanksgiving. You get to sit down with your family and friends and enjoy being together. Nothing brings people together like food and music. Those are two universal languages. We can be complete strangers, but if we eat together, we will find something to talk about.

   I love the idea of a day set aside to be thankful for what we have been blessed with. I love a day where the focus isn't on what else I can get, but how can I express gratitude for what I already have. I abhor the fact that the malls now open on Thanksgiving night! But that's okay; I stay home. (I'm too sore from all of that cooking anyway!)

If you're familiar with the love languages, my love language is acts of service. When I'm in the kitchen, it doesn't feel like a task or a chore. I'm putting my heart and soul into every dish I prepare. I want everyone who comes to my table, especially on a day of thanks, to taste love in every bite and morsel. I want them to taste the tenderness with which the greens were cooked down. I want them to taste the sweet touches of sugar in the biscuits; taste the honey kisses in the corn bread; taste the patience in the roasted sweet potatoes; taste how loved they are. The smiles on faces and the ease that comes across the room as everyone's belly starts to get full makes me smile. It makes my heart happy. It's how I say, "I love you."

SAUSAGE AND MUSHROOM DRESSING

*A*s long as I can remember, dressing has been my favorite side dish at Thanksgiving. It's hard for me to eat traditional dressing on any day that isn't Thanksgiving. So when I get a hankering for dressing the other 364 days of the year, this is what I make. It's still dressing, but the sausage and portobello mushrooms switch it up just enough.

Directions

1. Preheat oven to 375 degrees F.
2. In a large skillet, melt butter over medium-high heat. Add onion, celery, mushrooms, and garlic. Season with salt, pepper, and chili powder and cook until soft.
3. Add sausage and continue cooking until sausage is done. Turn off stovetop and remove the skillet from the heat.
4. Add bread crumbs to sausage mixture and stir, adding chicken broth until bread crumbs have absorbed the liquid and are no longer dry.
5. When bread crumbs have reached desired consistency, add eggs and combine well.
6. Transfer mixture to a 9-by-13 baking dish and bake for 40–45 minutes.

Serves 6–8

INGREDIENTS

½ cup (1 stick) butter
1 cup chopped yellow onion
1 cup chopped celery
¾ cup baby portobello mushrooms, chopped
2 cloves garlic, chopped
1 tablespoon salt
1 tablespoon pepper
1 teaspoon chili powder
1 pound hot italian sausage
1 pound sweet italian sausage
4 cups dry bread crumbs
2 cups chicken broth
2 eggs, lightly beaten

GARLIC AND HERB POTATO STACKS

*A*s with most of my recipes, you can tailor this to your family. Don't be afraid to experiment with different flavors. Make 'em Cajun-style, BBQ-style, or with lemon pepper. Don't be confined to just one option. Let your imagination run wild.

Directions

1. Preheat oven to 375 degrees F. Grease a muffin pan well.
2. Place sliced potatoes in a large bowl.
3. In small bowl, combine remaining ingredients. Pour over potatoes.
4. Stack the seasoned potato slices into the individual muffin cups of the prepared pan.
5. Bake in oven for 45–55 minutes, until a fork or toothpick goes all the way through.
6. Let potatoes rest for approximately 5–7 minutes before removing from muffin cups.

Serves 6–8

INGREDIENTS

- 6 medium yukon gold potatoes, peeled and sliced ⅛ inch thin
- 4 tablespoons butter, melted
- 4 tablespoons olive oil
- 3 tablespoons herb seasoning
- 1 tablespoons garlic, minced
- 1 teaspoon garlic powder
- 2 teaspoons kosher salt
- 1 teaspoon black pepper
- 1 cup shredded parmesan cheese

TIP

★ A mandolin makes thin-slicing the potatoes easy and sizes them consistently. But if you don't have one, just use a good knife and take your time.

MAMA'S POTATO SALAD

My mama's potato salad was and is legendary. You know how at every church, there's that lady who makes the bomb potato salad? Well, in my world, that was my mama. I ain't gon' lie; every now and then, someone would try to top her—usually a newcomer who didn't know. I felt a little bad for them, though, because when they weren't looking, folks would sneak into the church kitchen and say, "Don't give me that new stuff. I want Sis Johnson's potato salad!"

I asked my mom where she got her recipe because I have never found a recipe like hers. She says she loved potato salad as a child, so when she became an adult, she set out to learn to make one of her favorite dishes. Through trial and error and identification of what she tasted and liked, she landed on her perfect recipe.

I love watching her make it. Why? Because she can't really tell you what she does or how much of anything she puts in it. She just looks at it and says, "It looks a little dry to me" or "Hand me some more mustard, baby" or "I don't taste the celery like I want to." And when she finishes working her magic, *bam!*

When my husband and I started throwing parties together, I finally got bold enough one day to try making my mama's potato salad. I was scared because, like I told you, there's no real recipe for it. But she talked me through it, and it was pretty good. It wasn't hers, but I was pleased with the results.

I asked my husband to taste to it. Now, my Shane is brutally honest. He is not a mean man, but he will tell you the truth. He had a look of hesitation and apprehension on his face before he tasted it. I asked why. Then the funniest thing happened. He explained to me that his mom was the potato salad lady where he grew up!

We both laughed at the irony of our mothers on different coasts being the potato salad lady. He warned me that he didn't like anybody's potato salad except for his mama's. So I was prepared for a nice rejection of what I had made. Mind you, I had tasted what I made, and I was happy with it.

Being the good husband that he is, he tasted it. And he liked it! He made a new declaration that day that he would eat two potato salads—his mom's and my mom's. Prior to that, he wouldn't eat anybody else's potato salad . . . just his mom's. Period. End of story. Don't bother asking. He's still like that, except now it includes mine/my mom's.

I did my best to capture her potato salad in a recipe. Fingers crossed!

My mother - 1960

MAMA'S POTATO SALAD

Serves 10–12

Some people like onions in their potato salad; just remember that onions can sour your salad as they sit. Make sure you cook the potatoes until you can poke a toothpick all the way through them. If the potatoes are undercooked, the salad will be chunky, not smooth. Now if you want a chunky potato salad, that's the ticket. But if you don't want it chunky, cook them potatoes until they're soft (not mashed potatoes, just soft potatoes).

INGREDIENTS

- 3 pounds Russet potatoes, peeled
- 8 hard-boiled eggs, diced, plus 2 sliced hard-boiled eggs for garnish
- 6 stalks celery, chopped
- 1 large green bell pepper, chopped
- ⅓ cup McCormick's Salad Supreme seasoning
- 2 teaspoons salt
- 1 tablespoon paprika, plus more for garnish
- 3 tablespoons sweet pickle relish
- 1 tablespoon yellow mustard
- 1½ cups mayonnaise

Directions

1. In a large pot, bring water to a boil. Add potatoes and cook until a toothpick can go all the way through them.
2. Drain potatoes and allow to cool (otherwise, they'll be too hot to handle).
3. Dice potatoes into a large bowl. Fold in hard-boiled eggs, celery, and bell pepper. Combine well.
4. Add McCormick's seasoning, salt, and paprika. Ensure seasonings are distributed throughout the whole salad.
5. Fold in pickle relish, mustard, and mayonnaise. Combine well. Taste to be sure you like it. If you're not smiling, add a little more seasoning and taste again.
6. Garnish salad with sliced hard-boiled eggs and paprika sprinkles.
7. Refrigerate for several hours before serving for best results.

SWEET STUFF

I have an unrelenting sweet tooth. Dessert is probably my favorite meal of the day—and yes, I called it a meal because I plan dessert with the same care and concern as breakfast, lunch, and dinner. That makes it a meal.

Oddly enough, I've never been much of a chocolate fan, but that is rapidly changing. I've discovered a new love for semisweet chocolate that has me craving this rich, delectable delicacy like never before.

Each member of my family has a different favorite dessert. Since my goal is to keep them all smiling, I've gotten pretty good at a wide variety of sweets. But don't get it twisted. I don't make pretty cakes. It's just too time-consuming and precise. You gotta follow the recipe for best results, and I like to follow my heart. I hope your heart finds something it likes in these pages.

CLASSIC 7UP CAKE

This is my basic go-to pound cake recipe. It's not technically a pound cake, since it's not made with a pound of butter and such. But it works as the backdrop to a lot of things. You can serve this cake with fresh berries, whipped cream, and a simple glaze, or you can eat it like my kids like to eat it: all by itself!

Directions

1. Preheat oven to 325 degrees F. Spray a Bundt cake pan well with baking spray.
2. In a large bowl, cream butter and sugar together with an electric mixer until smooth and creamy.
3. Add eggs one at a time, ensuring each egg is fully incorporated before adding the next one.
4. Add lemon extract and combine well.
5. Add cake flour and 7UP, alternating, ⅓ at a time. Beat until just combined.
6. Pour cake batter into prepared pan. Bake for approximately 1 hour 15 minutes, until a toothpick inserted into the center of the cake comes out clean.
7. Let cake rest for 10 minutes before removing it from the pan.

MAKES 1 BUNDT CAKE

INGREDIENTS

3 sticks butter, softened

3 cups white sugar

5 eggs

2 tablespoons lemon flavor

3 cups cake flour

¾ cup 7UP brand soda

 TIP

★ This is 7UP Cake, and you need 7UP to make it—not Sprite, not lemon-lime soda, 7UP. Some things just are what they are. This is one of those things from the 'Bama side of the house. So trust me and use 7UP.

SWEET POTATO PIE

Makes 2 pies

This was the first dish I made as an adult that let me know I had the touch. My grandma makes the best sweet potato pies I've ever had (to this day). So when I moved from California to Virginia, mission #1 was to make a sweet potato pie that would make her proud. And baby, I did it. Even my daddy said this pie was good!

INGREDIENTS

3 pounds sweet potatoes

½ cup (1 stick) butter

1 cup brown sugar

1 cup white sugar

1 teaspoon nutmeg

1 teaspoon cinnamon

1 teaspoon vanilla

½ cup sweetened condensed milk

2 eggs

2 (9-inch) piecrusts, refrigerated or homemade (see Lori's No-Mess Perfect Piecrust, page 229)

Directions

1. Roast sweet potatoes in a 425 degree F oven for approximately 1 hour to 1 hour 15 minutes, until they are soft and mashable. Remove sweet potatoes and lower oven temperature to 325 degrees.
2. Peel sweet potatoes, add to a bowl, and mash.
3. Stir in butter, sugars, nutmeg, cinnamon, and vanilla. Mix well.
4. Add sweetened condensed milk and eggs. Mix well.
5. Pour batter evenly into pie shells.
6. Bake pie in oven for 1 hour 15 minutes until done (a toothpick or a knife should come out clean).

TIP

★ When you bake this pie, be sure to cover the edges while baking. Leaving the edges exposed for the entire cooking time will cause them to burn. Place some aluminum foil around the edges to cover them up, and all will be well.

BOURBON PEACH COBBLER

Serves 8

*P*each cobbler is another one of those classic comfort foods that make you smile. I remember craving it when I was carrying my oldest son. I think that's why he enjoys it so much now. There's nothing particularly different or special about this recipe, just the love and tenderness you put into every step.

Directions

1. Preheat oven to 375 degrees F.
2. In a large bowl, combine all filling ingredients.
3. Line bottom of a 10-by-10-inch or 9-by-13-inch baking dish with piecrust. Pour filling into crust.
4. Cover with second piecrust cut lattice-style, or cover entirely (like my grandma used to do). Brush top crust with egg wash.
5. Bake in oven until done, 45–60 minutes.

INGREDIENTS

For the filling:

- 3 cups peaches (fresh, canned, or frozen)
- 1 cup brown sugar
- ½ cup white sugar
- 4 tablespoons melted butter
- 1 tablespoon cinnamon
- 1 tablespoon nutmeg
- 1 teaspoon vanilla extract
- 3 tablespoons cornstarch
- ¼ cup bourbon

For the crust:

- 2 (9-inch) piecrusts, refrigerated or homemade (see Lori's No-Mess Perfect Piecrust, page 229)
- egg wash (1 egg plus 2 tablespoons water)

TIP

★ I usually use canned peaches in my peach cobbler. It's just easier!

CHOCOLATE LAVA CAKE

Makes 4 individual cakes

F've never been much of a chocolate fan, but something about this lava cake changed that. I will admit, it can be intimidating to bake a lava cake because precision is required (and it could still come out wrong). But when you master this type of elegance in your own kitchen, you'll pat yourself on the back.

Directions

1. Preheat oven to 450 degrees F.
2. In a microwave-safe bowl, combine chocolate chips and butter. Microwave in 30 second intervals, stirring between each. Combine until smooth.
3. Add cinnamon, vanilla, coffee crystals, salt, eggs, and egg yolks. Combine well.
4. Spoon in flour and combine well, but do not overmix.
5. Spray ramekins very well with baking spray. (I mean seriously—spray the heck out of them!)
6. Spoon mixture into ramekins evenly. Fill each one approximately ⅔ full.
7. Bake in oven for exactly 10 minutes. Remove from oven.
8. When cool to the touch, turn ramekins upside down to release. Garnish as desired.
9. Serve immediately to get the full effect of the molten center—and don't forget the vanilla ice cream!

INGREDIENTS

For the cakes:

- 1 cup semisweet chocolate chips
- 5 tablespoons unsalted butter
- 1 teaspoon cinnamon
- 1 teaspoon vanilla
- ½ teaspoon instant coffee crystals
- ¼ teaspoon salt
- 2 eggs
- 2 egg yolks
- ¼ cup all-purpose flour

For garnish:

- powdered sugar
- whipped cream
- raspberries
- toasted coconut flakes

MADDIE'S APPLE CARAMEL COBBLER

It never fails: when I bake an apple cobbler, I rarely get a piece! My family devours it before I know what happened. Served the cobbler warm with vanilla ice cream and the caramel sauce the apples are baked in—but make sure you get a piece first!

Directions

Make the caramel sauce:

1. In a small saucepan, combine the brown sugar and half-and-half. Heat over medium heat until the brown sugar dissolves.
2. Remove saucepan from heat and add butter and vanilla. Stir to combine and set aside to cool while you prepare the apple filling.

Make the apple filling:

1. Preheat oven to 375 degrees F.
2. In a large bowl, toss apple pieces with lemon juice (see tip.)
3. Add brown sugar, cornstarch, cinnamon, and nutmeg. Combine until apples are coated.

Assemble the cobbler:

1. Place one piecrust on the bottom of a 9-by-9-inch baking dish.

SERVES 10

INGREDIENTS

For the caramel sauce:

- 1 cup brown sugar
- ¼ cup half-and-half
- 4 tablespoons butter
- 1 teaspoon vanilla

For the apple filling:

- 7 large granny smith apples, cut into bite-size pieces
- 1 tablespoon lemon juice
- ½ cup brown sugar
- 3 tablespoons cornstarch
- 1 teaspoon cinnamon
- 1 teaspoon nutmeg

For assembling the cobbler:

- 2 tablespoons all-purpose flour
- 2 (9-inch) piecrusts, refrigerated or homemade (see Lori's No-Mess Perfect Piecrust, page 229)
- 2 tablespoons melted butter
- 1 tablespoon white sugar

TIPS

- When cutting apples, remember: not too small and not too large! I like to cut them into cubes or thin slices. As long as you can get the piece in your mouth without choking, you're good to go.
- Did you know that lemon juice will prevent apples from turning brown? Yup! When you slice up your apples, toss in the lemon juice.
- Sprinkling flour on the crust at the bottom of the cobbler will ensure that as the apple filling cooks and liquid is created with the melting sugar, the crust won't get soggy. Nobody wants a soggy-bottom cobbler!

2. Sprinkle flour on top of bottom piecrust, then top with apple filling.
3. Cover filling with second piecrust. Brush with melted butter and sprinkle with white sugar.
4. Using a knife, cut slits in top crust to allow steam to escape as the cobbler bakes.
5. Bake cobbler in the oven for 45–55 minutes, until the crust is golden brown.

NANA JO'S OLD-FASHIONED LEMON PIE

Makes 1 (9") pie

INGREDIENTS

For the crust:

1 ¼ cup ginger snaps (about 25)

½ cup (1 stick) butter, melted

¼ cup sugar

For the filling:

3 eggs yolks

1 (14-ounce) can sweetened condensed milk

½ cup lemon juice

As with most things in my cooking world, church continues to play a big role. When I moved to Virginia, I quickly got involved in another church community and was right at home. My expanded world included a lot of the same comforts that make home the best place in the world. Enter Nana Jo. Nana Jo was one of the first people I met when I moved to Virginia. She quickly earned a special place in my heart, and over the years, she has become one of the greatest treasures in my life. She is the definition of a classic and contemporary church lady—and her pie demonstrates that!

Directions

1. Preheat oven to 350 degrees F.
2. Crush gingersnaps into fine crumbs using a food processor, or just crush them in a plastic bag.
3. Add melted butter and sugar to cookie crumbs and stir well until crumbs are moistened.
4. Press the cookie crumbs into the bottom of a 9-inch pie plate.
5. Bake the gingersnap pie shell on 350 degrees for 8 minutes. Remove from oven and set aside to cool.
6. Reduce oven heat to 325 degrees.
7. In a medium bowl, combine egg yolks, sweetened condensed milk, and lemon juice. Whisk ingredients together well.

8. Pour filling into the pie shell. Return to oven and bake at 325 degrees for 30 minutes.

9. Remove from oven and allow pie to set for several hours (overnight in refrigerator is best).

PUMPKIN BROWN-SUGAR POUND CAKE

Makes 1 Bundt cake

When fall starts knocking at our door, we welcome the season with this cake. I love baking pound cakes because they are very forgiving. You can play with the ingredients, within reason, and still obtain a good result. This cake came about from one of my playing-with-pound-cake sessions. Move over, pumpkin-spice latte—there's a new player in town!

INGREDIENTS

For the cake:

- 3 sticks salted butter, softened
- 2 ¾ cups brown sugar
- ½ cup white sugar
- 5 eggs
- ½ cup pumpkin puree
- 1 teaspoon vanilla
- 1 teaspoon cinnamon
- 1 teaspoon nutmeg
- 1 teaspoon ground cloves
- 1 teaspoon ground ginger
- 3 cups cake flour
- ¾ cup whole milk

For the glaze:

- 1 (14-ounce) can sweetened condensed milk
- 1 cup brown sugar
- 4 ounces cream cheese
- 1 teaspoon vanilla

Directions

Make the cake:

1. Preheat oven to 325 degrees F. Spray a cake pan well with baking spray.
2. In a large bowl, combine butter and sugars. Cream with an electric mixer until smooth and creamy.
3. Add eggs one at a time, ensuring that each egg is fully incorporated before adding the next.
4. Add pumpkin puree, vanilla, cinnamon, nutmeg, cloves, and ginger.
5. Add cake flour and whole milk, alternating, ⅓ at a time. Beat until just combined.
6. Pour batter into prepared pan. Bake in oven for approximately 1 hour 10 minutes, until toothpick inserted into the center of the cake comes out clean.
7. Let cake rest for 10 minutes before removing from the pan.

Make the glaze:

1. In a saucepan, combine all glaze ingredients except vanilla. Heat over low to medium heat. When well combined and thickened, remove from heat and add vanilla.
2. Once thickened and well incorporated, drizzle hot glaze onto cake.

OLD-FASHIONED RICE PUDDING

Serves 4–6

INGREDIENTS

1⅓ cups water
½ cup uncooked white rice
½ teaspoon salt
2 cups whole milk
2 egg yolks, beaten
½ cup sugar
1 teaspoon vanilla
¼ cup raisins (optional)
nutmeg and cinnamon, for sprinkling on top

This is another of my mom's classic recipes. I absolutely love when she makes this; for some reason, it just makes me smile. Don't rush the process of cooking the rice. After all, it is rice pudding! Take your time and cook the rice, add the milk, and so forth. You'll be glad you did.

Directions

1. Preheat oven to 350 degrees F. Spray a 9-by-9-inch baking dish well with baking spray.
2. In a medium saucepan, bring water to a boil. Stir in rice and salt. Cover and simmer until water is absorbed, about 30 minutes.
3. Add milk and bring mixture to a gentle boil. Stir continuously until mixture thickens.
4. In a medium bowl, with a whisk, combine egg yolks, sugar, and vanilla.
5. Slowly add the egg mixture to the rice mixture. Be sure to go slow so the heat from the rice mixture doesn't scramble the eggs. Add a little and stir . . . add a little more and stir.
6. Stir in raisins, if using.
7. Transfer mixture to prepared baking dish and bake in oven for 45–50 minutes, until a toothpick or a knife inserted in the center comes out clean.
8. Sprinkle with nutmeg and cinnamon before serving.

BANANA PUDDING

SERVES 8–10

*T*his is my husband's favorite dessert. I have one rule that I share with all of my newlywed girlfriends: whatever your husband likes, get real good at fixin' it! And that's exactly what I've done. Traditionally, meringue is put on top of banana pudding, but now that I'm a grown up, I like to use whipped cream. Both are absolutely delicious; it really depends on your mood! Try it both ways and see what you like best.

INGREDIENTS

2½ cups sugar

2 (12-ounce) cans evaporated milk

6 tablespoon all-purpose flour

4 egg yolks, beaten

4 tablespoons butter

1 teaspoon vanilla

5 bananas, sliced

1 box vanilla wafer cookies

whipped cream or Meringue (page 231), for topping

Directions

1. In a medium saucepan, over medium heat, combine sugar, evaporated milk, and flour. Continue stirring until mixture becomes thick enough to coat the back of a spoon, about 20 minutes. Be sure to keep stirring so the mixture doesn't burn or stick.

2. Add egg yolks to milk mixture slowly, stirring constantly. Don't rush the process or you'll get scrambled eggs.

3. Once eggs have been fully incorporated, remove pan from heat. Stir in butter and vanilla.

4. In a 9-by-13-inch baking dish, assemble the banana pudding in layers starting with custard, then vanilla wafers, then bananas. Continue until all ingredients are used, finishing with vanilla wafers on top.

5. Crush any remaining vanilla wafer cookies and reserve the crumbs. Refrigerate and top with whipped cream and reserved crumbs when chilled.

 TIP

★ Chill overnight in refrigerator for best results. If you can't wait that long, at least 3–4 hours.

★ You can also top with meringue from the egg whites instead of whipped cream. That's the old fashioned way!

WHITE CHOCOLATE CRÈME BRÛLÉE

Makes 5–6 servings

INGREDIENTS

1 cup white chocolate chips

4 egg yolks

¼ cup white sugar, plus extra sugar for caramelization on top

1 teaspoon vanilla

1½ cup heavy whipping cream

*A*s with other elegant dishes, this jazzed-up crème brûlée may seem intimidating to prepare at home. But it's easier than you think. If you're not a fan of white chocolate, add milk chocolate. Oh . . . and for an extra dash of class, add a splash of Grand Marnier!

Directions

1. Preheat oven to 300 degrees F.
2. Melt white chocolate either on stovetop or in microwave. If melting in microwave, heat in 30-second intervals, stirring between each. If melting on the stovetop, continue stirring so the white chocolate doesn't stick or burn. Set aside.
3. In a large bowl, combine egg yolks and sugar with a wire whisk. When well combined, stir in the vanilla and continue whisking to combine well.
4. In a medium saucepan over medium heat, bring the heavy whipping cream almost to a boil but not quite. The edges should begin to simmer.
5. Slowly incorporate the hot whipping cream into the egg yolk mixture, being sure not to scramble the eggs. Keep whisking the entire time.
6. Stir in the white chocolate and combine well.
7. Pour batter evenly into ramekins. Use a measuring cup to ensure that you are including the same amount in

each ramekin. This will ensure even baking time as well as even proportions.

8. Place ramekins in a baking dish deep enough to hold all the ramekins and hot water to be added in the next step.

9. Pour hot water into baking dish with ramekins, creating a water bath. Pour water to halfway up the side of ramekins.

10. Bake for 35–45 minutes, until set. The top should be jiggly but not runny.

11. Remove from oven and cool to room temperature, about 30 minutes. Refrigerate for at least 3 hours to allow custard to finish setting.

12. Once custard is fully cooled and set, sprinkle the top of each ramekin with approximately 1 tablespoon sugar. Caramelize using a kitchen torch or by placing ramekins under the broiler for 3–5 minutes (keep an eye on them).

BAKE-SALE PIES

Years ago, when life was much simpler, there were bake sales. A lot has changed since then. It's not so safe anymore to just buy baked goods in front of a grocery store from people you don't know. But back in the day, it was everything! Our church used to have bake sales frequently, typically in front of a now-defunct store called Gemco. (I wonder what ever happened to Gemco. I think, through a serious of purchases, it became Target.)

Anyway, our bake sales consisted of two pies: coconut cream and lemon meringue. Sometimes there would be sweet potato pies, but 99.9 percent of the time, it was coconut cream and lemon meringue. To this day, I have a special affinity for these two pies.

I remember so vividly the church mothers taking pies out of the oven and whipping meringue. The worst part about bake sales was, you couldn't eat the pies. You couldn't even sneak a slice! The whole pie had to be pretty, which made it look even more appealing, and then you couldn't even touch it. That is torture for an eight-year-old.

I would hope and pray that my mama would buy a pie so I could eat it. Sometimes I'd get lucky; since my granddaddy was the pastor, my grandma could take home a pie for him. If that happened, I could get a slice. But that was a rare occasion.

Sadly, they never gave me the recipes for those pies. I think that's because they never had one. They just knew how to cook. I've done some research and found some pretty decent substitutes, but some days, I would give anything to smell and taste those bake-sale pies again.

COCONUT CREAM PIE

Makes 2 (9") pies

Church-lady pies! Bake-sale pies! I love these old-school pies. They just bring a smile to your face, and they taste like home.

Directions

1. Preheat oven to 350 degrees F.
2. Blind bake piecrust in oven for 20–25 minutes until light golden brown. Remove from oven and reduce heat to 325. (See page 229, for instructions on blind baking.)
3. Meanwhile, in a medium saucepan, whisk together sugar and cornstarch. Slowly add milk, turn heat to medium, and continue stirring until mixture gets thick.
4. Remove from heat and slowly add egg yolks. Be sure to take your time so you don't scramble the eggs. Stir constantly.
5. Place the pan back on heat and continue cooking until mixture thickens, stirring constantly. Stir in vanilla and coconut flavoring. Stir in butter until melted. Fold in coconut flakes.
6. Pour custard into the baked pie shell. Spread meringue on top. Be sure to seal all of the edges between the meringue and the piecrust.
7. Sprinkle 2 tablespoons shredded coconut on top of the meringue.
8. Bake pie 15–20 minutes until coconut is toasted and meringue is a light golden brown.

INGREDIENTS

- 2 (9-inch) piecrusts, refrigerated or homemade (see Lori's No-Mess Perfect Piecrust, page 229)
- 1 cup sugar
- ⅓ cup cornstarch
- 2¼ cups whole milk
- 4 egg yolks
- 1 teaspoon vanilla
- 1 teaspoon coconut flavoring
- 2 tablespoons butter
- 1 cup sweetened coconut flakes, plus 2 tablespoons for topping
- Meringue (page 231)

LEMON MERINGUE PIE

Serves 8

*A*nd another church pie! This was my favorite growing up. I could eat these nonstop—except my mama wouldn't let me!

Directions

1. Preheat oven to 350 degrees.
2. *Make the meringue*: In the bowl of a stand mixer, combine egg whites and cream of tartar. Beat until foamy. Slowly incorporate sugar and continue beating. Add vanilla and beat until stiff white peaks form.
3. Blind bake piecrust in oven for 20–25 minutes, until light golden brown. Remove from oven and reduce heat to 325.
4. In a medium saucepan, whisk together sugar and cornstarch. Slowly add water, turn heat to medium, and continue stirring until mixture gets thick.
5. Remove from heat and slowly add yolks. Be sure to take your time so you don't scramble the eggs. Stir constantly.
6. Place the pan back on heat and continue cooking until mixture thickens, stirring constantly. Stir in vanilla, lemon zest, and lemon juice. Stir in butter until melted.
7. Pour custard into baked pie shell. Spread meringue on top. Be sure to seal all of the edges between the meringue and the pie crust.
8. Sprinkle 2 tablespoons shredded coconut on top of the meringue.
9. Bake pie 15–20 minutes until coconut is toasted and meringue is a light golden brown.

INGREDIENTS

2 (9-inch) piecrusts, refrigerated or homemade (see Lori's No-Mess Perfect Piecrust, page 229)

1½ cups sugar

⅓ cup cornstarch

1½ cups water

3 egg yolks

1 teaspoon vanilla

zest and juice (about ½ cup) of 1 lemon

3 tablespoons butter

2 tablespoons sweetened coconut flakes

CHOCOLATE BREAD PUDDING WITH IRISH WHISKEY CARAMEL CREAM SAUCE

Everybody loves a good bread pudding. Add chocolate, whiskey, and caramel, and you've got a new classic. We typically enjoy this on St. Patrick's Day. It's my ode to Irish food (you know, the Irish whiskey part). The whiskey isn't overpowering but adds amazing dimension to the flavor of the sauce. Because you cook down the alcohol for ten to fifteen minutes, this is safe for kids to consume. If you'd like to make it a little more "adult," boil the alcohol for less time and add extra whipped cream to get the consistency to where you want it.

Directions

Make the bread pudding custard:

1. Cut bread into cubes and allow to sit out for 30–45 minutes to dry out slightly (or place in oven at 250 degrees for approximately 15 minutes).
2. In a large bowl, whisk together eggs, half-and-half, sugars, cocoa, vanilla, and instant coffee.
3. Place bread cubes in a 9-by-13-inch baking dish, sprinkling chocolate chips throughout.
4. Pour the custard mixture over the bread cubes and chocolate chips. Allow custard to soak into the bread cubes for at least 30 minutes before baking. This

Serves 6

INGREDIENTS

For the bread pudding custard:

- 1 pound italian bread
- 5 eggs
- 2 cups half-and-half
- ¾ cup white sugar
- ¾ cup brown sugar
- 1 tablespoon cocoa powder
- 1 teaspoon vanilla
- 1 teaspoon instant coffee (or espresso)
- 1 cup semisweet chocolate chips

For the Irish whiskey caramel cream:

- 1 stick unsalted butter
- 1 cup brown sugar
- 1 cup Bailey's Irish Creme
- 1 cup Irish whiskey
- ½ cup heavy whipping cream

ensures that all of the cubes are moistened with the custard. When nearly ready to bake, preheat oven to 350 degrees.

5. Bake bread pudding in preheated oven for 35–45 minutes, until a knife comes out clean.

Make the Irish whiskey caramel cream:

1. In a medium saucepan, melt butter over medium heat and then stir in brown sugar. Once combined, slowly add the Irish crème and whiskey. Combine well.
2. Keep to a steady boil for 10–15 minutes to allow the alcohol and the liquid to reduce.
3. Stir in heavy whipping cream.

Assemble the dessert:

1. When bread pudding comes out of oven, immediately pour hot cream caramel sauce over pudding so it can absorb sauce.

Baked with Love

CHOCOLATE WAFFLES

Makes 5 large waffles

These are as rich and decadent as you are imagining they are. I like to serve them with whipped cream and chocolate syrup. I mean, if you're going to make a chocolate waffle, you might as well fix it up. You will need a waffle maker for these. Trust me—you'll get plenty of use out of it.

Directions

1. In a large bowl, combine flour, sugar, cocoa, baking powder, baking soda, and salt.
2. In a separate bowl, combine eggs, butter, vanilla, and buttermilk.
3. Combine dry and wet ingredients with a spoon. Batter should be lumpy. Don't overmix it. Let it stay slightly lumpy.
4. Cook according to waffle maker manufacturer's instructions.

INGREDIENTS

2 cups all-purpose flour

½ cup sugar

⅓ cup cocoa powder

1 tablespoon baking powder

1 teaspoon baking soda

1 teaspoon salt

2 eggs, lightly beaten

4 tablespoons butter, melted

1 teaspoon vanilla

2 cups buttermilk

★ For plain waffles, substitute an additional ⅓ cup flour for the ⅓ cup of cocoa powder. It's that easy!

CHOCOLATE CHIP SKILLET COOKIE

Makes 1 (8" or 10") cookie

$\mathcal{S}$ometimes you just need a cookie. One of my dearest friends used to say she was just going to "go eat a cookie!" She was so right. This cookie is made in a cast-iron skillet, and you can leave the center a little gooey—that makes it taste even better! A big scoop of vanilla ice cream makes it just right.

INGREDIENTS

½ cup butter
½ cup brown sugar
¼ cup white sugar
1 egg
1 teaspoon vanilla
1 cup flour
¼ teaspoon baking powder
¼ teaspoon baking soda
¾ cup semisweet chocolate chips

Directions

1. Preheat oven to 350 degrees F.
2. In an 8- or 10-inch cast-iron skillet, melt the butter over medium heat. Add both sugars. Stir to combine.
3. Place skillet in refrigerator or freezer for 10–15 minutes to cool.
4. When the skillet has cooled, add the egg and vanilla to the sugar mixture. Combine well.
5. Stir in the flour, baking powder and baking soda. Combine well.
6. Stir in chocolate chips and be sure they are evenly distributed throughout the skillet.
7. Bake for approximately 25–30 minutes.

★ If you want this baked firm like a more traditional cookie, cook it an additional 5–7 minutes.

OOEY-GOOEY CAST-IRON CHOCOLATE CARAMEL BROWNIE

Makes 1 (8") skillet brownie

INGREDIENTS

- ½ cup (1 stick) butter
- 1 cup semisweet chocolate chips
- 2 eggs
- ½ cup sugar
- 2 teaspoons vanilla
- 2 teaspoons instant espresso (or coffee)
- ⅓ cup all-purpose flour, plus 1 tablespoon for caramel baking chips
- 1 teaspoon baking powder
- ½ teaspoon salt
- ½ cup caramel baking chips

Something about baking desserts in cast-iron skillets makes them taste even better. This brownie is no exception. I load it up with caramel chips (and sometimes white chocolate chips and toffee and . . . you get the picture) for even more decadence. Be sure to add some instant coffee or espresso to enhance the flavor of the chocolate. You will thank me!

Directions

1. Preheat oven to 350 degrees F.
2. Melt butter and semisweet chocolate chips either on the stovetop or in the microwave. If melting in the microwave, heat in 30-second intervals, stirring between each interval. If melting on the stovetop, continue stirring so the chocolate doesn't stick or burn.
3. In a large bowl, combine eggs, sugar, vanilla, and instant espresso. Combine ingredients well but don't overmix.
4. Pour melted chocolate into egg mixture. Pay attention to the temperature of the melted chocolate as you incorporate; if the chocolate is too hot, you can accidentally scramble the eggs. Keep stirring the whole time you add the chocolate to ensure no cooked eggs.

5. With a fine mesh sieve, sift in flour, baking powder, and salt. Stir well to combine.

6. In a medium bowl, toss the caramel baking chips with 1 tablespoon flour. Fold the caramel chips into the brownie batter (the flour will keep them from sinking to the bottom).

7. Pour brownie batter into a cast-iron skillet and bake for 25 minutes.

8. Remove and enjoy immediately with ice cream. The inside will be gooey but oh so delicious.

LORI'S NO-MESS PERFECT PIECRUST

Makes 2 (9") piecrusts

INGREDIENTS

3 cups all-purpose flour

⅓ cup sugar

1 teaspoon salt

1 cup shortening

1 egg yolk

6–10 tablespoons ice-cold water

I have experimented with a lot of piecrust recipes over the years. This is by far my favorite one. I tweaked and tweaked until I got it just right, and it never fails. The egg yolk makes the crust silky smooth, and the shortening makes it nice and flaky.

Directions

1. In a large bowl, whisk together flour, sugar, and salt.
2. Cut in shortening and use your hands to crumble the ingredients together. The consistency should be like peas. You can also use a pastry cutter, but I have always found that my two hands do this better than any kitchen gadget.
3. Using your hands, work in the egg yolk.
4. Add cold water to the dough 1 tablespoon at a time. Start with 6 tablespoons and combine. Continue adding water 1 tablespoon at a time until the dough begins to form a ball.
5. Split the dough in half and transfer the balls of dough to two separate sheets of plastic wrap.
6. Cover each piecrust dough ball with another sheet of plastic wrap.
7. Using a rolling pin, form each ball into a round disc and flatten to ⅛ of an inch. Wrap them each in plastic wrap and place in the refrigerator until ready to use.
8. To blind bake the crust, poke fork holes in the bottom of the crust and bake on 350 degrees F for 25 minutes until crust is light golden brown.

MERINGUE

MAKES ENOUGH TO TOP **1** PIE

INGREDIENTS

4 egg whites
½ teaspoon cream of tartar
⅓ cup sugar
1 teaspoon vanilla

 TIP

★ Cream of tartar helps egg whites beat up big and fluffy. They also stabilize the meringue to keep it from collapsing. If you don't have cream of tartar, lemon juice or white vinegar can also aide in the stabilization of the meringue. The last thing you want is for your meringue to crumble.

*I*f you're wondering why the meringue is sitting here all by itself, it's because meringue works with a lot of different desserts, including lemon meringue pie, coconut cream pie and banana pudding. So rather than give the recipe over and over, I'm just gonna put it right here.

Directions

1. In a stand mixer, beat egg whites and cream of tartar for several minutes until they look foamy.
2. Slowly add in sugar, 1 teaspoon at a time, and continue beating.
3. Add vanilla and continue beating until stiff peaks form. When you hold the mixture up with a spoon or your whisk, it should remain upright and not fall over.
4. Spread on top of pie and bake on 350 degrees for 15–20 minutes until light golden brown.

BREADS

I don't know which section is my favorite: sweets or bread. I've decided that they are pretty much the same thing. Basically, my favorite thing is anything carbohydrate! From biscuits to corn bread to waffles, I just can't get enough of the stuff.

My oldest son is the same way. I'm not sure if that's a good thing or a bad thing. He's always up for some garlic bread with dipping oil. I've decided that as long as he and I can bond over the goodness that comes from flour and gluten, I'll always have my (biggest) baby! That's my story, and I'm sticking to it.

GARLIC HERB CHEESE BREAD

> **SERVES 4–6**

INGREDIENTS

1 stick melted butter

½ cup extra virgin olive oil

3 tablespoons parsley

2 tablespoons basil

2 tablespoons garlic, minced or chopped

1 teaspoon salt

1½ cups shredded cheese

1 pound fresh bread (round loaf)

This is probably one of my daughter's favorite appetizers. Actually, all three of my kids get excited when I pull out a fresh round from the bakery. This recipe is pretty simple, but I've discovered the technique of placing oil and herbs between the cuts really gets the flavor fully incorporated. For an extra burst of flavor, use a rosemary and olive oil loaf. Wow!

Directions

1. Preheat oven to 350 degrees F.
2. In medium bowl, combine butter, olive oil, parsley, basil, garlic, salt, and cheese. Set aside.
3. Cut bread from the top down into squares, but do not cut all the way through to the bottom of the bread.
4. Transfer the bread to a baking sheet. Place the butter mixture into each cut of the bread. Top with cheese.
5. Cover with foil and bake 10–15 minutes until warm and cheese has melted.

ZESTY LEMON BLUEBERRY SCONES

Makes 2 dozen

Great for breakfast time, teatime, snack time, any time! Scones make you feel fancy, and they're super easy to make. I encourage you to experiment with different flavors and such. You can add a tablespoon of thyme or ginger and liven up the lemon even more.

Directions

1. Preheat oven to 375 degrees F.
2. In a large bowl, whisk together flour, sugar, baking powder, and salt (if using).
3. Cut in the butter and combine with pastry cutter or your hands until crumbly.
4. In a small bowl, combine the egg, whipping cream, and lemon extract and mix well. Add to the dry ingredients.
5. Add zest and lemon juice and combine wet and dry ingredients well.
6. Place the dough on a floured surface and bring together with a light knead. Don't overdo it here. You just want to bring it all together.
7. Fold in blueberries.
8. Roll out dough to approximately 1–2 inches thick.
9. Cut into desired shapes.
10. Place scones on a baking sheet and bake for 15–18

INGREDIENTS

For the scones:

- 3 cups all-purpose flour
- ⅔ cup sugar
- 2 tablespoons baking powder
- ½ teaspoon salt (if unsalted butter)
- 1 cup butter
- 1 egg
- 1 cup heavy whipping cream
- 1 teaspoon lemon extract
- zest and juice of 1 lemon
- 1 cup fresh or frozen blueberries

For the glaze:

- 1–2 cups powdered sugar
- 4–5 tablespoons heavy whipping cream
- 1 teaspoon vanilla
- lemon juice

minutes. Remove from oven and allow to cool slightly before glazing.

11. ***Make the glaze:*** Whisk or sift powdered sugar into a medium bowl. Add whipping cream 1–2 tablespoons at a time until mixture achieves desired thickness. Add vanilla and a splash of lemon juice and combine well.

I NEED SOME STRENGTH

My grandma could cure anything in the kitchen. It didn't really matter what was ailing you—whether it was your body hurting or just your feelings—she could fix it in the kitchen. She was an educated teacher, a devoted wife and mother, and the church mother. You couldn't outwork her. It's like she was made from some sort of super Teflon or something that just let her keep going. She was the first Energizer bunny I ever saw.

But every now and then, she would get tired or sick and have to shut it down for a few days. Most ladies from the Deep South figure out how to read their own tea leaves. So she knew if her knee hurt a certain way, she couldn't stand up too much this week. Or if her back was a little sore, she couldn't cut up those greens today. When she felt a cold coming or just felt her body was weak and tired, she would make some "strength."

Now I was the one grandchild who thinks she knows everything about Grandma, but the first time she told me about this strength, I was perplexed. You see, we talked pretty much every day, usually multiple times a day. That's just how we were. One day on the phone, I said my typical, "Hi, Grandma, how you doing?"

Grandma going to church!

Her reply this particular day: "The old lady not feeling the best. But I'm gon' be all right, baby. I fixed me some strength, and I believe I'm startin' to feel better already."

Me: "Grandma, what is *strength*?"

Grandma: "I fried me some corn bread, baby. You know corn bread can make you better."

Me: "Grandma, you have never told me that before."

Grandma: "I haven't? Well, baby, I been doin' this for years."

And that was that. I had to be in my teenage years when this conversation took place, but I remember it like it was yesterday. As much as I love corn bread, and as good as I think my corn bread is, I can't get my fried corn bread to taste like hers. I'm missing something. But I did find a way to make it all right for my family and me.

Enter corn fritters. I love making them, and while they aren't Grandma's fried corn bread, they sho do make you feel better. How do I know? My daughter said one day, "Mommy, I just ate a bunch of corn fritters, and I feel so much better."

Grandma was right!

My grandma - 1960

SWEET BUTTERMILK CORN BREAD

Serves 6–8

INGREDIENTS

1 cup yellow cornmeal

1 cup all-purpose flour

¼ cup white sugar

2 teaspoons baking powder

½ teaspoon baking soda

1 teaspoon salt

1½ cups buttermilk

3 tablespoons salted butter, plus melted butter for topping

1 egg

1 cup fresh or defrosted frozen corn (optional)

Corn bread is one God's best inventions (if you ask me). It can make pretty much any meal better. I like my corn bread a little sweet, which is why I use so much sugar. If you're not a fan of sweet corn bread, just lessen the sugar . . . or better yet, use honey instead.

Directions

1. Preheat the oven to 400 degrees F. Grease a 9-by-13-inch baking dish well (cooking spray is okay).

2. In a large bowl, combine cornmeal, flour, sugar, baking powder, baking soda, and salt.

3. In a separate bowl, combine buttermilk, butter, and egg.

4. Add the buttermilk mixture to the cornmeal mixture; do not overmix. The batter should be lumpy.

5. Fold corn into batter (if using).

6. Add batter to prepared baking dish. Bake until an inserted toothpick comes back clean, about 35 minutes.

7. Remove from oven and top with melted butter.

BUTTERMILK BISCUITS

MAKES 12–15 BISCUITS

A comfort-food cookbook is incomplete without a biscuit recipe. This one is no exception. I love biscuits like nobody's business, so of course, I had to include my basic buttermilk biscuit. I like to mix some cake flour with the self-rising flour to get lighter biscuits, but you really can't go wrong however you make these.

INGREDIENTS

- 2 cups self-rising flour
- 2 tablespoons baking powder
- ½ teaspoon baking soda
- ¼ teaspoon salt
- ½ cup cold butter, plus 2–3 tablespoons melted butter for topping
- 1 cup cold buttermilk

Directions

1. In a large bowl, whisk together flour, baking powder, baking soda, and salt.
2. Cut in cold butter with a pastry cutter or a fork, or just use your fingers. Mix until mixture is like pebbles.
3. Slowly pour in cold buttermilk. Stir to combine. Dough will be sticky, so be sure to use a floured surface when you empty it from the bowl to knead.
4. Knead dough 4–6 times. Be careful not to overknead the dough, so the biscuits stay light and fluffy. Spread the dough out about ¾ inch thick and cut biscuits.
5. Place cut biscuits on an ungreased baking sheet and place in freezer while preheating oven to 425 degrees F, 10–15 minutes.
6. When oven reaches 425 degrees, remove biscuits from freezer and top with melted butter. Bake in oven for 15 minutes.
7. When the biscuits come out of the oven, immediately pour more melted butter on them.

TIP

★ The key to big fluffy biscuits is using cold ingredients when preparing the dough, then making sure everything is nice and cold before it goes into the oven. I don't preheat my oven until I place the biscuits in the freezer. That way, I know they have at least 10 minutes to get cold before the oven is ready.

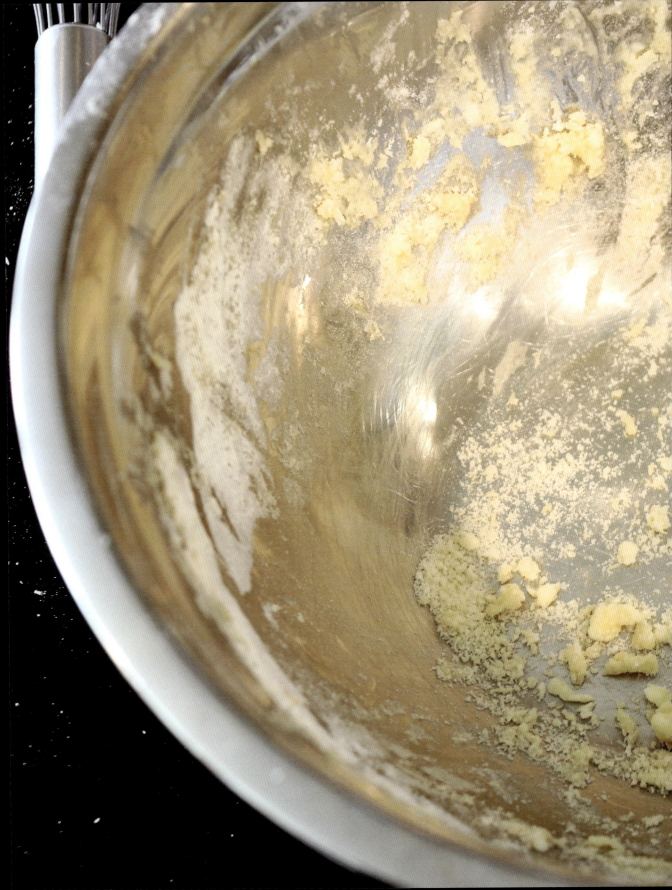

PANCAKES

I have always been a carbohydrate lover. Breads and french fries have always made me happy. When I was little, I would spend summers, holidays, and long weekends with my grandparents who lived across town. My grandfather was our church's pastor and my grandmother was a teacher. She cooked seven days a week, no exception. But I was a picky eater. And there were really only about two things I wanted her to fix for me: biscuits and pancakes.

She wouldn't make me biscuits that often. I think they were too much hassle! But she would make me pancakes in a heartbeat. Here's the catch: she wouldn't make me pancakes when she fixed dinner. She didn't play that. Dinner was fixed, and you needed to eat it (or at least sit at the table and play with your food). However, around nine in the evening (especially in the summer), when we got home Bible study, if I asked correctly, with just the right amount of sad eye, she'd make me pancakes for a snack before bed.

Those were the best pancakes in the world! I think what made them so good was how she fried them in a little oil. My mama made big, smooth, pretty pancakes. Grandma's pancakes weren't as big or as smooth, but they had a little tang from the oil.

When I got to be a teenager, I remember making pancakes for my daddy one day. My daddy could give my mama a hard time about how she fixed something this time versus that time, but don't get it twisted. He didn't want anybody else's cooking except for hers, and he loved Mama's pancakes. So when I stepped up to make pancakes, I made them like Grandma, fried in a little oil. He tasted it and said, "These are pretty good—a little tangy! I like that. This how your grandma make them?"

By this time, everybody knew how I was about my grandma's cooking.

"Yup!" I beamed with pride at his approval. And that was that. I can make pretty pancakes like my mama (and they taste good!), but when it's just me, fried in a little oil is the way to go.

BUTTERMILK PANCAKES

Makes 10–12 pancakes

I could live on pancakes. It might become a boring existence, but I could do it. You're wondering again, I'm sure: *Why is there a recipe for pancakes in this cookbook?* The answer is simple: this is my life in food, and buttermilk pancakes have always been a big part of my life. I just love 'em. Add some blueberries, whipped cream, or whatever else strikes your fancy. Comfort food is all about feeling good!

INGREDIENTS

2 cups all-purpose flour

2 tablespoons white sugar

2 teaspoons baking powder

1 teaspoon baking soda

1 teaspoon salt

2 cups buttermilk

2 eggs

4 tablespoons shortening

Directions

1. In a large bowl, whisk together flour, sugar, baking powder, baking soda, and salt.
2. In a separate bowl, whisk together buttermilk and eggs. Be sure to fully incorporate the eggs into the buttermilk.
3. Pour buttermilk mixture into flour mixture. Stir to combine.
4. Add shortening and combine. Do not overmix. Batter should be slightly lumpy.
5. Cook pancakes on griddle over medium heat until done.

 TIP

★ When the batter has bubbles on top of it, it's time to flip the pancakes. Keep an eye on them so they don't burn.

LEMON STUFFED FRENCH TOAST

*T*his is more of that easy everyday elegance I enjoy so much. These are perfect for Easter brunch or Christmas morning breakfast. You can create pretty much any flavor profile you like to for the filling. You can probably tell by now that I really like lemon. But don't be stuck just 'cause I am. Do you!

Directions

1. *Make the lemon cream cheese filling:* Combine all filling ingredients in a bowl with a fork or whisk—or in a stand mixer—until smooth. Be sure the cream cheese is soft, or this will be next to impossible.

2. *Make the custard:* Combine the custard ingredients in a shallow bowl and mix well. Set aside for dipping the bread.

3. Cut a pocket in top of each bread slice, stopping approximately 1 inch from the bottom of the bread. (Do not cut too far down, or your filling will ooze out.) Fill the pocket with the lemon cream cheese mixture.

4. Dip each filled slice in custard and cook on griddle at low temperature (approximately 300 degrees) until outside is done and inside is warm.

Serves 6

INGREDIENTS

For the lemon cream cheese filling:

- 8 ounces softened cream cheese
- ⅓ cup powdered sugar
- 3 tablespoons lemon juice

For the french toast custard:

- ½ cup heavy whipping cream
- 6 eggs
- 1 teaspoon all-purpose flour
- 3 tablespoons sugar
- 2 teaspoons cinnamon
- 1 teaspoon vanilla
- 1 loaf brioche french bread, cut into slices 1½–2 inches thick

TIP

★ Be sure to cook the french toast on a low temperature. You want to make sure you give the filling a chance to get warm. Don't rush the process, or you'll have hot toast with cold filling. That's not cool!

RED VELVET WAFFLES

Makes 4 large waffles

I don't know if I think these are a Christmas food or a Valentine's Day food. Truth is—they work for both. They are so elegant and beautiful—once you drizzle them with cream cheese frosting or whipped cream, you'll be in heaven and you'll want a kiss. I guess that makes them a Valentine's Day item!

INGREDIENTS

2 cups all-purpose flour

¼ cup white sugar

2 tablespoons cocoa powder

3 teaspoons baking powder

1 teaspoon baking soda

1 teaspoon salt

2 eggs

1¾ cups buttermilk

2 teaspoons vanilla

2 ounces red food coloring

4 tablespoons shortening

Directions

1. In a large bowl, whisk together flour, sugar, cocoa, baking powder, baking soda, and salt.
2. In a separate bowl, combine eggs, buttermilk, vanilla, and food coloring.
3. Pour buttermilk mixture into flour mixture and combine.
4. Add the shortening. Do not overmix. Batter should be bumpy.
5. Cook in your waffle maker following the manufacturer's directions.

SPICY SAUSAGE GRAVY AND BISCUITS

SERVES 6

INGREDIENTS

½ pound mild ground sausage

½ pound sweet ground sausage

2 tablespoons garlic powder

2 tablespoons onion powder

1 teaspoon cayenne

1 tablespoon flour

2 tablespoons butter or olive oil (as needed)

3 cups half-and-half (milk or heavy whipping cream are also acceptable)

⅓ cup water (optional)

salt and black pepper to taste

biscuits (homemade, or buy some from the grocery store)

This is the kind of dish that makes your toes curl up, it's so good. The spiciness of the gravy against the smooth flavor of the buttermilk biscuits . . . I get excited just thinking about it!

Directions

1. In a large skillet, brown all the sausage over medium-high heat. When almost done, add garlic powder, onion powder, and cayenne. Mix well to stir seasonings into sausage.

2. Add flour to cooked sausage and stir until sausage has absorbed the flour. If additional moisture is needed, add butter or olive oil, 1 tablespoon at a time, until all flour is absorbed.

3. Once flour is fully absorbed, slowly pour in half-and-half. Add water, if desired, to break up the richness of the half-and-half. Season with salt and pepper.

4. Ladle sausage gravy over biscuits and eat yourself silly.

TIPS

★ If you want to thicken your gravy, dissolve additional flour in water (1 tablespoon flour at a time into approximately ¼ cup of water or half-and-half). Then pour the flour/liquid mixture into the boiling sausage gravy in skillet.

★ On the other hand, if you want to loosen your gravy, add ¼ cup water (or cream) with no flour and stir.

ABOUT THE AUTHOR

Lori "Chef Lorious" Rogers specializes in both classic and contemporary comfort food. Born in California and raised by a close-knit family anchored in southern tradition from Alabama, this "Calibama" girl learned very early that food cooked with love has the power to inspire and heal.

Chef Lorious has been cooking for her family and friends in her kitchen (more affectionately known as her "Love Lab") for almost two decades. She regularly shares her recipes and meal preparation ideas by conducting cooking demonstrations and sharing her culinary expertise through television programming in the Washington, DC metropolitan area and various social media outlets. You can catch her on Washington DC's "Good Morning Washington" (WJLA-ABC), "Good Day DC" (WTTG-FOX), and follow her on YouTube, Facebook and Instagram (@ChefLorious).

Chef Lorious is a devoted wife and mother of three beautiful children, and she especially enjoys serving her church family. She is grateful for the opportunity to take her message of loving others authentically through food to the masses. Whether cooking with her on screen or following her recipes, you are sure to feel the love that she has for both her community and for cooking!

INDEX

Apple Cobbler, Caramel, Maddie's, 191
Asian Wings, Sweet and Spicy, 23

Bacon
    Bacon Guacamole, 13
    Baked Potato and Bacon Soup, 41
    Corn, Bacon, and Potato Chowder, 43
    Sauteed Cabbage with Bacon and Garlic, 159
Bacon Guacamole, 13
Bacon, Baked Potato, Soup, 41
Bacon, Corn, and Potato Chowder, 43
Bacon, Sauteed Cabbage with Bacon and Garlic, 159
Baked Potato and Bacon Soup, 41
Bake-Sale Pies, 211
Banana Pudding, 205
Beef
    Beef and Sausage Meatloaf, 81
    Beef Stew, 53
    Beef Stroganoff, 87
    Calibama Chili, 55
    Chimichurri Steak Nachos, 29
    Country Fried Steak and Gravy, 101
    Crab-Topped Filet Mignon, 89
    Easy Everyday Beef Wellington, 95
    Extra Meaty Hearty Lasagna, 121
    Guinness Shepherd's Stew, 61
    Herb-Crusted Prime Rib, 99
    Steak and Cheese Egg Rolls, 17
Beef Stew, 53

Beef Stroganoff, 87
Beef Wellington, Easy Everyday, 95
Biscuits, Buttermilk, 247
Black-Eyed Peas, Lucky, 161
Blueberry, Zesty Lemon, Scones, 237
Bourbon Peach Cobbler, 187
Breads, 233–259
    Buttermilk Biscuits, 247
    Buttermilk Pancakes, 253
    Garlic herb Cheese Bread, 235
    Lemon Stuffed French Toast, 255
    Red Velvet Waffles, 257
    Spicy Sausage Gravy and Biscuits, 259
    Sweet Buttermilk Corn Bread, 245
    Zesty Lemon Blueberry Scones, 237
Bread Pudding, Chocolate, with Irish Whiskey Caramel Cream Sauce, 217
Brie, Baked, Sweet and Salty, 15
Broccoli Salad, Tangy, 35
Brown Sugar, Pumpkin, Pound Cake, 199
Brussels Sprouts, Crispy Glazed, 165
Buffalo Chicken Taquitos, 9
Buttermilk Biscuits, 247
Buttermilk Pancakes, 253

Cabbage, Sauteed, with Bacon and Garlic, 159
Cajun Chicken Pasta, 125
Cake, 7UP, Classic, 183
Caramel, Apple Cobbler, Maddie's, 191

Cheese Bread, Garlic Herb, 235
Chicken
    Buffalo Chicken Taquitos, 9
    Cajun Chicken Pasta, 125
    Chicken Pot Pie, 59
    Garlic Cream Chicken, 75
    Hearty Chicken Piccata, 79
    Lemon Basil Chicken, 123
    Lorious Chicken and Waffles, 69
    Rosemary Seared Chicken Thighs, 67
    Spicy Seafood, Chicken, and Sausage Stew, 49
    Sweet and Spicy Asian Wings, 23
Chicken and Waffles, Lorious, 69
Chicken Piccata, Hearty, 79
Chicken Thighs, Rosemary Seared, 67
Chicken, Garlic Cream, 75
Chili, Calibama, 55
Chimichurri Steak Nachos, 29
Chipotle Deep-Fried Macaroni and Cheese Balls, 11
Chocolate
    Chocolate Bread Pudding with Irish Whiskey Cramel Cream Seauce, 217
    Chocolate Chip Skillet Cookie, 223
    Chocolate Lava Cake, 189
    Chocolate Waffles, 221
    Ooey-Gooey Cast-Iron Chocolate Caramel Brownie, 225
    White Choclate Crème Brulee, 207

Chocolate Bread Pudding with Irish Whiskey Caramel Cream Sauce, 217
Chocolate Caramel Brown, Ooey-Gooey, Cast-Iron, 225
Chocolate Chip Skillet Cookie, 223
Chocolate Lava Cake, 189
Chocolate Waffles, 221
Coconut Crème Pie, 213
Collard Greens, Grandma's, 163
Cookie, Chocolate Chip Skillet, 223
Corn Bread, Sweet Buttermilk, 245
Corn Fritters, Calibama, 27
Corn, Bacon, and Potato Chowder, 43
Crab
    Crab Stuffed Flounder, 143
    Crab Topped Filet Mignon, 89
Crab-Stuffed, Flounder, 143
Crème Brulee, White Chocolate, 207

Desserts, 181–231
    Banana Pudding, 205
    Bourbon Peach Cobbler, 187
    Chocolate Bread Pudding with Irish Whiskey Caramel Cream Sauce, 217
    Chocolate Chip Skillet Cookie, 223
    Chocolate Lava Cake, 189
    Chocolate Waffles, 221
    Classic 7UP Cake, 183
    Coconut Cream Pie, 213
    Lemon Meringue Pie, 215
    Lori's No-Mess Perfect Piecrust, 229
    Maddie's Apple Caramel Cob, 191bler
    Meringue, 231
    Nana Jo's Old-Fashioned Lemon Pie, 195
    Old-Fashioned Rice Pudding, 203
    Ooey-Gooey Cast-Iron Chocolate Caramel Brownie, 225
    Pumpkin Brown-Sugar Pound Cake, 199
    Sweet Potato Pie, 185
    White Chocolate Crème Brulee, 207
Dip Dinners, 71

Egg Rolls, Steak and Cheese, 17
Enchiladas, Pork, Verde, 113

Filet Mignon, Crab-Topped, 89
Fish Fries, 129
Fish
    Crab-Stuffed Flounder, 143
    Blackened Salmon and Lemon Herb Butter, 137
    Pan-Seared Swordfish with Greek Sauce, 131
Flounder, Crab-Stuffed, 143
French Toast, Lemon Stuffed, 255

Garlic and Brown Sugar Pork Tenderloin, 77
Garlic and Herb Potato Stacks, 173
Garlic Cream Chicken, 75
Garlic Herb Cheese Bread, 235
Greens, Collard, Grandma's, 163
Guacamole, Bacon, 13
Guinness Shepherd's Stew, 61

Hearty Chicken Piccata, 79

I Love Me Some Grits, 139
I Need Some Strength, 241

Lamb Chops in Madeira Wine Sauce, 107
Lasagna, Extra Meaty Hearty, 121
Lemon
    Lemon Basil Chicken, 123
    Lemon Meringue Pie, 215
    Lemon Stuffed French Toast, 255
    Nana Jo's Old-Fashioned Lemon Pie, 195
    Zesty Lemon Blueberry Scones, 237
Lemon Basil Chicken, 123
Lemon Meringue Pie, 215
Lemon Pie, Nana Jo's, Old-Fashioned, 195
Lemon Stuffed French Toast, 255
Lemon, Zesty, Blueberry Scones, 237
Lobster and Shrimp Rolls, 147
Lobster, Creamy Cajun, Shrimp, Fettuccine, 133
Lori's No-Mess Perfect Piecrust, 229
The Love of My Life, 91

Macaroni and Cheese Balls, Deep Fried, Chipotle, 11
Macaroni and Cheese, Lorious, 153
Main Courses, 65–125
    Beef and Sausage Meatloaf, 81
    Beef Stroganoff, 87
    Cajun Chicken Pasta, 125
    Country Fried Steak and Gravy, 101
    Crab-Topped Filet Mignon, 89
    Easy Everyday Beef Wellington, 95
    Extra Meaty Hearty Lasagna, 121
    Garlic and Brown Sugar Pork Tenderloin, 77
    Garlic Cream Chicken, 75
    Hearty Chicken Piccata, 79

INDEX

Herb-Crusted Prime Rib, 99
Lamb Chops in Madeira Wine Sauce, 107
Lemon Basil Chicken, 123
Lorious Chicken and Waffles, 69
Lori's Meaty Marinara Sauce, 85
Pork Enchiladas Verde, 113
Rosemary Seared Chicken Thighs, 67
Sausage-Stuffed Portobello Mushroom Caps, 109
Smothered Pork Chops, 117
Mama's Potato Salad, 175
Mama's Potato Salad, 179
Marinara Sauce, Lori's Meaty, 85
Meatloaf, Beef and Sausage, 81
Meringue, 231
Mother's Day, 105
Mushroom Caps, Portobello, Sausage-Stuffed, 109

Pancakes, 249
Pancakes, Buttermilk, 253
Pasta
    Cajun Chicken Pasta, 125
    Chipotle Deep Fried Macaroni and Cheese Balls, 11
    Creamy Cajun Lobster and Shrimp Fettuccine, 133
    Extra Meaty Hearty Lasagna, 121
    Lorious Macaroni and Cheese, 153
    Lori's Meaty Marinara Sauce, 85
Peach Cobbler, Bourbon, 187
Pie
    Coconut Crème Pie, 213
    Lemon Meringue Pie, 215
    Lori's No-Mess Perfect Piecrust, 229
    Meringue, 231
    Nana Jo's Old-Fashioned Lemon Pie, 195
    Sweet Potato Pie, 185

Pork
    Bacon Guacamole, 13
    Baked Potato and Bacon Soup, 41
    Corn, Bacon and Potato Chowder, 43
    Garlic and Brown Sugar Pork Tenderloin, 77
    Pork Enchiladas Verde, 113
    Sausage and Mushroom Dressing, 171
    Sausage Tortellini Soup with Spinach, 45
    Sausage-Stuffed Portobellow Mushroom Caps, 109
    Smothered Pork Chops, 117
    Spicy Sausage Gravy and Biscuits, 259
    Spicy Seafood, Chicken and Sausage Stew, 49
    Sweet Potato Pie, 185
Pork Chops, Smothered, 117
Pork Enchiladas Verde, 113
Pork Tenderloin, Garlic and Brown Sugar, 77
Potato
    Baked Potato and Bacon Soup, 41
    Garlic and Herb Potato Stacks, 173
    Mama's Potato Salad, 179
    Potato, Corn, Bacon, Chowder, 43
Potato Salad, Mama's, 179
Potato Stacks, Garlic and Herb, 173
Pound Cake, Pumpkin Brown-Sugar, 199
Prime Rib, Herb-Crusted, 99
Pumpkin Brown-Sugar Pound Cake, 199

Red Velvet Waffles, 257

Refined Little Palates, 155
Rice Pudding, Old Fashioned, 203
Rosemary Seared Chicken Thighs, 67

7UP Cake, Classic, 183
Salmon, Blackened, with Lemon Butter, 137
Sausage and Mushroom Dressing, 171
Sausage Tortellini Soup with Spinach, 45
Sausage, Beef, Meatloaf, 81
Sausage, Spicy Seafood, Chicken, Stew, 49
Sausage, Spicy, Gravy and Biscuits, 259
Sausage-Stuffed Portobellow Mushroom Caps, 109
Scones, Zesty Lemon Blueberry, 237
Seafood, 127–149
    Blackened Salmon with Lemon Herb Butter, 137
    Cilantro Lime Shrimp Tacos, 149
    Crab-Stuffed Flounder, 143
    Creamy Cajun Lobster and Shrimp Fettuccine, 133
    Lobster and Shrimp Rolls, 147
    Pan-Seared Swordfish with Greek Sauce, 131
    Spicy Shrimp and Grits, 141
Shrimp
    Cilantro Lime Shrimp Tacos, 149
    Creamy Cajun Lobster and Shrimp Fettuccine, 133
    Lobster and Shrimp Rolls, 147
    Shrimp Po-Boy Dip, 37
    Spicy Seafood, Chicken, and Sausage Stew, 49
    Spicy Shrimp and Grits, 141
Shrimp and Grits, Spicy, 141
Shrimp Po'Boy Dip, 37

Shrimp Tacos, Cilantro Lime, 149
Shrimp, Creamy Cajun Lobster, Fettuccine, 133
Shrimp, Lobster Rolls, 147
Sides, 151–179
- Crispy Glazed Brussels Sprouts, 165
- Garlic and Herb Potato Stacks, 173
- Grandma's Collard Greens, 163
- Lorious Macaroni and Cheese, 69
- Lucky Black-Eyed Peas, 161
- Mama's Potato Salad, 179
- Sausage and Mushroom Dressing, 171
- Sauteed Cabbage with Bacon and Garlic, 159

Small Plates and Starters, 7–37
- Bacon Guacamole, 13
- Buffalo Chicken Taquitos, 9
- Calibama Corn Fritters, 27
- Chimichurri Steak Nachos, 29
- Chipotle Deep-Fried Macaroni-and-Cheese Balls, 11
- Shrimp Po'Boy Dip, 37
- Smoky Spinach Dip, 25
- Steak-and-Cheese Egg Rolls, 17
- Sweet and Salty Baked Brie, 15
- Sweet and Spicy Asian Wings, 23
- Tangy Broccoli Salad, 35

Smoky Spinach Dip, 25
Smothered Pork Chops, 117
Soups, 39–63
- Baked Potato and Bacon Soup, 41
- Beef Stew, 53
- Calibama Chili, 55
- Chicken Pot Pie, 59
- Corn, Bacon, and Potato Chowder, 43
- Guinness Shepherd's Stew, 61
- Sausage Tortellini Soup with Spinach, 45
- Spicy Seafood, Chicken, anmd Sausage Stew, 49
- Turkey Tortilla Soup, 63

Spicy Seafood, Chicken and Sausage Stew, 49
Spinach Dip, Smoky, 25
Spinach, Sausage Tortellini Soup, 45
Steak and Cheese Egg Rolls, 17
Steak Nachos, Chimichurri, 29
Steak, Country Fried, and Gravy, 101
Summer BBQs, 31
Super Bowl, 19
Sweet Buttermilk Corn Bread, 245
Sweet Potato Pie, 185
Sweet Stuff, 181–231
- Banana Pudding, 205
- Bourbon Peach Cobbler, 187
- Chocolate Bread Pudding with Irish Whiskey Caramel Cream Sauce, 217
- Chocolate Chip Skillet Cookie, 223
- Chocolate Lava Cake, 189
- Chocolate Waffles, 221
- Classic 7UP Cake, 183
- Coconut Cream Pie, 213
- Lemon Meringue Pie, 215
- Lori's No-Mess Perfect Piecrust, 229
- Maddie's Apple Caramel Cobbler, 191
- Meringue, 231
- Nana Jo's Old-Fashioned Lemon Pie, 195
- Old-Fashioned Rice Pudding, 203
- Ooey-Gooey Cast-Iron Chocolate Caramel Brownie, 225
- Pumpkin Brown-Sugar Pound Cake, 199
- Sweet Potato Pie, 185
- White Chocolate Cream Brulee, 207

Swordfish, Pan-Seared, with Greek Sauce, 131

Taquitos, Buffalo Chicken, 9
Thanksgiving, 167
Tortellini Soup, Sausage, Soup with Spinach, 45
Turkey Tortilla Soup, 63

Vegetables
- Calibama Corn Fritters, 27
- Crispy Glazed Brussels Sprouts, 165
- Grandma's Collard Greens, 163
- Lucky Black-Eyed Peas, 161
- Sauteed Cabbage with Bacon and Garlic, 159
- Smoky Spinach Dip, 25
- Tangy Broccoli Salad, 35

Waffles
- Chocolate Waffles, 221
- Red Velvet Waffles, 257

White Chocolate Crème Brulee, 207
Wings, Asian, Sweet and Spicy, 23